DIARY OF AN UNKNOWN

EUROPEAN SOURCES

Russell Epprecht, Series Editor

DIARY
OF AN
UNKNOWN

Jean Cocteau

A NEW TRANSLATION BY
Jesse Browner

PARAGON HOUSE PUBLISHERS

NEW YORK

First American edition, 1988

Published in the United States by
Paragon House Publishers
90 Fifth Avenue
New York, NY 10011

Library of Congress Cataloging-in-Publication Data

Cocteau, Jean, 1889–1963.
  [Journal d'un inconnu.   English]
  Diary of an unknown / Jean Cocteau ; a new translation by Jesse
Browner.
    p.   cm.
  ISBN 1-55778-061-7
  I. Title.
PQ2605.015J613 1988
855'.912—dc19   87-35944
                                                             CIP

We who know what this gesture attracts,
Abandon the dance and the drinkers of wine . . .

Opera

CONTENTS

Contents

INTRODUCTION

With *Diary of an Unknown* (1953), Jean Cocteau takes up that most French of all literary forms, the *essay*. Indeed, so conscious is he of using a medium new to him, and of the difficulty of adapting it to his own idiosyncracies, and so conscientious is he in adhering to its exalted traditions, and so diligent in bringing the fact to the attention of his readers, that no introduction could avoid the comparison, which Cocteau so obviously longed for, with the genitor of its form, Montaigne's *Essays*.

Combining personal experience, classical erudition, and a certain mellifluence of style, the essay allows an author the freedom to expatiate on a variety of subjects and ideas that owe their interrelatedness solely to the quality of the author's imagination. To this extent, the essay seems particularly suited to older writers seeking to establish a philosophical or metaphysical (or, in Cocteau's terms, "metapsychical") unifying thread with which to bind up the wealth of a life's experience. Montaigne claims that his life and his *Essays* are "consubstantial." As with many other masters with whom he sought to identify himself (most notably Picasso and Stravinsky), Cocteau's admiration for Montaigne overflows into emulation, and thus *Diary of an Unknown* becomes one of the strongest "consubstantiations" of his life and work that Cocteau ever produced, and perhaps the most paradoxical.

Cocteau evidently found that he had a great deal in common with Montaigne. Like Montaigne, after a lifetime in the public eye, he "retired" to the countryside to write his essays. Just as Montaigne had lost his cherished friend Etienne de la Boétie to an untimely death, Cocteau had lost his beloved Raymond Radiguet, and like Montaigne, his grief over the loss had colored the rest of his life, and he took charge of posthumously publishing his friend's greatest work. Like Montaigne, he prided himself on his "capacity for independence and absolute resistance when essential principles were involved."[1] Like Montaigne, whose retirement was frequently interrupted by social demands and military service, Cocteau's "retirement" was forever being interrupted by his "skirmishes" with the public and the press. And, like Montaigne, he continually harps on his lack of memory.

We should not be surprised, then, to find that Cocteau's essays scrupulously fulfill the formal, thematic, and even syntactical demands of the genre. Like Montaigne's, they are semi-autobiographical, though not necessarily intended to provide anecdotal fodder to a curious public. Instead, the author's aim is to coax from the fruit of personal experience the seeds of truth ubiquitous in human endeavor and intercourse. To this end, formal rhetorical structuring becomes obsolete, and in fact Cocteau chooses to develop the style of Montaigne's earlier essays—a style designed to mimic the rambling sequence of thoughts and ideas that spring to the mature, well-educated mind in contemplation of its own symmetry. In their respective essays "On Friendship," Montaigne and Cocteau come very near to empathy in this regard.

Any determined effort to establish more than an incidental resemblance in the two authors' temperaments, however, quickly breaks down. For if Montaigne, in his own casual way, could be said to possess intellectual symmetry, then Cocteau could be more accurately described as hysterically assymetric. That is much more in keeping with the Cocteau known to generations of admirers and detractors alike, and the aspect of his character that makes *Diary of an Unknown* such a fascinating study in paradox and contradictions.

Diary of an Unknown was first published ten years before the poet's death at age 74. Its basic subject matter is developed from ideas first touched on in his published diary, *Le passé défini,* which he wrote at the same time (and which we are fortunate enough to have in a recent translation by Richard Howard, *Past Tense*).[2] It was written during his "retirement," the years he spent living (with his "adopted" son, the actor Edouard Dermit) as a guest at the Villa Santo Sospir, home of his friend and patron Francine Weissweiller. This final period might be said to begin with his autobiographical *The Difficulty of Being* (1947) and to end with his death. Though it may be his least prolific period, however, it should by no means be interpreted as any sort of "twilight," as many tend to do. In *Past Tense*, he relates (p. 273) Jean Genet's accusation that "You've done nothing but be a star for ten years." Yet this is patently untrue: the ten years prior to that had seen, amongst other accomplishments, his creation of two cinematic masterpieces, *Beauty and the Beast* (1945) and *Orpheus* (1950), as well as the brilliant stage-play *The Human Voice* (1947). Furthermore, as Cocteau himself points out in his vivid and ingenuously merciless analysis of François Mauriac in the essay "On a Purple Passage," his work was still capable of causing a scandal in 1952, and he of still emerging victorious from that scandal. Of course, Cocteau remains outwardly demure: "A man attacked at the Champs-Elysées roundabout must defend himself, even if it sickens him." And it is in his lifelong pursuit of such publicity that Cocteau most emphatically and irrevocably parts ways with Montaigne, and defines himself as Cocteau.

There are two commonplaces inevitably brought up in reference to Jean Cocteau. The first is that his life was part of his art. The second is that even those who have never encountered his work seem to know—or believe they know—something about him. There is a certain degree of truth to both statements, owing to the fact that they are strongly interrelated.

Despite his many claims to the contrary, Jean Cocteau, throughout his entire lifetime, attracted and solicited public attention with the assiduity of a politician, and in his talent for publicity was rivalled only by the Surrealists, who may well have perfected this art by his example. His final press conference, on the occasion of the death of Edith Piaf, was given only hours before his own death. Furthermore, his fame was hardly confined to the arts: his name, his face, and his exploits—side by side with practically every artistic celebrity of the twentieth century—regularly found their way into the popular press, where they became familiar to generations who had never seen one of his plays, his films, his ballets, or his exhibitions, who had never read one of his novels, his poetry, or his journalistic and critical works.

His wrangles with his contemporaries were notorious, and the enemies he made amongst them invariably illustrious. One of his earliest was Serge Diaghilev, who had been inclined to like the star-struck young poet, and to show him favor. But the friendship cooled when the impresario learned that, among other things, Cocteau was frequenting the backstage of the Ballets Russes to help give Vaslev Nijinsky, Diaghilev's lover, his rubdowns between performances. Diaghilev's hatred persisted through the decades, so much so that it was he who engineered Cocteau's ouster from the 1952 revival of *Oedipus Rex* which Cocteau discusses in "On an Oratorio." Then there was André Gide, whose smoldering antipathy was fanned to enmity when he suspected Cocteau of seducing one of his young protegés. (In "On a Justification for Injustice," Cocteau claims that Gide was simply paranoid: "I knew Gide and his almost feminine jealousy . . . Gide confessed, and admitted that he had wanted to kill me.") Stravinsky grew to find Cocteau's

Introducción

correspondence "irritating and futile," while Picasso came to avoid his company whenever possible. (It is characteristic of Cocteau to call their kindnesses to him "reconciliations," and to publicize them as such.) André Breton led the cabal of Surrealists that vilified and persecuted Cocteau (in the 1920s, one of them reportedly called Cocteau's mother to say her son was dead), and their public invective against him was never more bitter than when his star was waxing and theirs was waning. Besides his personal enemies, who were all past masters of publicity in their own rights, Cocteau had other eccentricities that kept him newsworthy: he was a well-known homosexual in a deeply homophobic society, a self-proclaimed opium addict, and was even (unjustly) accused of collaborating with the Nazis during the German occupation of Paris. Few of these elements escaped the public eye, and if they did, Cocteau was there to set the record straight. After he had published his *Lettre à Jacques Maritain* (1926) to announce his return to the Catholic church, he complained that it was not received with the controversy he felt it deserved. Even the Paris secret police knew him primarily as *"Cocteau, Jean.* Opium addict. Pederast. (Says he is a poet.)"[3]

It is natural, therefore, that the public at large came to see him as nothing but the sum of his press releases and scandals, and to assume that his works (less visible to the majority of the public than his flamboyant demeanor) were simply extensions of such publicity. Natural, too, that often scandalized bourgeois opinion should be carried over by its representatives in the press (in France, as elsewhere, the ruling contingent) to the critique of his art, which to their refined sensibilities often seemed scarcely less scandalous. There is therefore a threefold mythification at work in contemporary accounts of his work and life: his own deliberate self-mythification, engineered in part to protect his private life (such as it was), and in part to develop his mystique; the mythification of a general public that saw little but his outlandish behavior and statements; and the mythification of critics riding the wave of popular bias. Cocteau was to cultivate such mythification (while decrying the mythomaniacs) all his life, and so was directly or indirectly responsible for the problems we continue to have today in pinning him down. Indeed, like James Joyce, the idea of keeping the critics busy for the next fifty years would probably have delighted him to no end.

To a certain extent, *Diary of an Unknown* recapitulates these familiar aspects of Cocteau. Those readers already familiar with his work will find well-known Coctelian themes broached again and again—angels, invisibility, the treachery of colleagues and supposed friends, advice to the young, the birth of ideas. Those readers who are picking him up for the first time may be struck by his persistent reference to himself (not all that unusual in the essay form), and by his apparently flippant way of tackling universals, but the essays all stand up perfectly well on their own and require no prior knowledge or preconceptions of the author to be accessible and entertaining. Nevertheless, along with *The Difficulty of Being*, the book seems to mark a turning point, not only in Cocteau's career but in his personal evolution as well, and to this extent provides insights into the writer that, at the very least, come as a surprise to those who felt they knew his work and persona well.

Most of Cocteau's works written during his last ten years are characterized by a tendency towards introspection, and a perhaps overly defensive need for self-justification. *Diary of an Unknown* marks a time in which his reflections turn increasingly upon those aspects of his life which he has found the least acceptable because of the confusion they have sown both in himself (Cocteau had always been driven by his insecurity and a need to find favor amongst those who were least prone to bestow it) and in others, such as Gide and Breton, who clung to ancient prejudices and continued to judge him by a standard set forty years earlier.

Cocteau writes, "Man seeks to escape himself in myth, and does so by any means at his disposal. Drugs, alcohol, or lies. Unable to withdraw into himself, he disguises himself. Lies and inaccuracy give him a few moments of comfort . . ." The impression, as we shall often see in this book, is that Cocteau may be using an exterior subject (in this case, "man") to chastise himself for a lifetime of self-mythologizing. "Fabulization" and "idolization" are the strongest recurring themes in the book, and that they should have such personal connotations for Cocteau can only mean that they were uppermost in his mind as he thought about himself during the course of its composition. It was a time in which Cocteau's life (as Richard Howard writes in his "Translator's Note" in

Past Tense) had "fallen upon the thorns of its own creative impulse."

The result is a work beset by intrinsic contradictions, as Cocteau struggles to reject his insecurities while yet remaining deeply vulnerable to the attacks and prejudice to which he continued to be subject. He had always made a show of welcoming such attacks as proof of his ethical righteousness ("One is either judge or accused. The judge sits, the accused stands. Live on your feet."), and he continued to feel the necessity of receiving such blows (even to the point of exaggerating or inventing them), while resenting them as unjust but mitigating them as unwitting kindnesses all the same. He is well aware of the paradoxes which these irreconcilable yearnings engender (in *Past Tense*, he says, "In the *Journal d'un inconnu* there are snarls I am incapable of disentangling"), but, typically, he glosses over them by emphasizing them: "I consider contradiction to be the very soul of day-to-day scholarship, and that it is honest not to correct one's errors." Believing himself to have covered all the bets, Cocteau has unknowingly laid himself wide open, much more revealingly than in any "confession" he might *choose* to make.

And so it was two years later, in 1955, when he was compelled to justify seeking and accepting a seat in the Academie Française, the most conservative of the institutions representing the Establishment he had always belittled, and that had always belittled him. "Since it is now unfashionable to join the Academy," he says, "I have remained a rebel by joining it."

Again, we see the threefold mythification at work as Cocteau attempts to juggle personal, popular, and critical demands that are untenable. In many ways, such paradox is the very essence of *Diary of an Unknown*—contained, in fact, within the title itself.

Perhaps fittingly, such confusion is most evident here in his exploration of sexuality, at a time when his own sexual activity may have been slowing down or have come to a halt. Cocteau had always regarded Freudian theory as simplistic, appealing only to those for whom sex was "pivotal," and he does not hesitate to call Freud a "plunderer of poor tenements." Yet, he devotes an entire chapter ("On Criminal Innocence") to a psychosexual case history which he analyzes in purely Freudian terms. Further, the book is dotted here and there with gruesome little Freudian vignettes involving sexual repression and castration. What this may indicate is that, in his declining years, Cocteau was beginning to evaluate his own sexuality in the light of a theory he had always rejected, and that he was finding—almost despite himself, and to his great discomfiture, or so it seems—that it held some validity in his case.

He reacts similarly when discussing homosexuality (one must presume his own). His sympathy naturally lies with the repressed, and one of the most moving passages in the book is one in which he describes the humiliations of young homosexuals, at the hands of the police, that have led some to commit suicide. He also exalts "Greek love" as "simply erotic intimacy between pupil and master [that] had nothing to do with powerful bonds of the soul," which had been precisely his lifelong experience, most of it with himself in the role of "master." And yet, above and beyond this, he exalts a type of friendship stripped of such attachments as the highest possible embodiment of human bonding—a type of friendship, it should be added, that he was never to experience in the depth of feeling with which he describes it. Again, we find a confusion between conflicting values—those that the author has held all his life, and those that are creeping up on him in his maturity. As harbingers of old age, they may be unwelcome, but they cannot be ignored.

This confusion has seeped into the very fiber of the writing, into Cocteau's own voice, which at times sings in the taut countertenor of his youth, and at others strains to find the lush baritones of mature wisdom. Compare the trippingly tongue-in-cheek prose of "On a Cat Story" ("There appeared four white cats and four black cats, bearing swords and felt hats and . . . walking on their hind legs, and carrying on their shoulders a little coffin, on top of which rested a little gold crown") with the tendentious, self-important, and almost incomprehensible stylizations of the amateur metaphysician in "On Distances": ". . . a dizziness that does not exclude the possibility of a gravitational mechanics driven by acquired force." Yet again, we find a Cocteau drawn towards something he does not quite understand, and of which he is not quite sure he approves.

As we have seen, Cocteau is not at all unaware of what is happening. Mixed in with the stock phrases of self-deprecation is some truly insightful commentary on his own plight: "I blindly pile up boulders of unreason." "I aspire to it without understanding it, and never will understand it." But to what extent does this awareness lead to a wholesale reevaluation of his life's work? Has Cocteau actually reached the point of repudiating his past? These are the questions that *Diary of an Unknown,* unlike any other of Cocteau's works, raises in all seriousness, and at least partially answers.

Poets, says Cocteau, are "guided by wise caution to hide their souls' shamelessness beneath a stylized disguise." In other words, the carnival procession of his life, all the public bluster and fanfare, were intended as a smoke screen to mask the deeply subversive truths of his work. This much is the old Cocteau line, the "robust narcissist"[4] who, in the words of Henri Ghéon, "must not be surprised if . . . we are embarrassed by the pose he affects, and if we try to consider his poems apart from his fame."[5] There is much of this old Cocteau in *Diary of an Unknown,* a man who, rather than be embarrassed by his affectedness, will most unblushingly and engagingly boast of it.

But there is a new, "unknown" Cocteau here, one who is testing the waters of an unfamiliar sensibility by first immersing his subjects, rather than himself, into them. "What does a painter do to highlight the mistakes in the portrait he is painting?" he asks. "He inverts them in a mirror," and Cocteau has used *Diary of an Unknown* as his looking glass, a process in which, coming full circle, he rejoins Montaigne at last. And it is fair to say that he does not always like what he sees. When he wrote that a "mystery is always spun out when hypocrisy can feast itself in the name of humanness," he could not have failed to apply the same litmus test to his own life. What he seems finally to have come to recognize is that, in protecting himself behind his "stylized disguise," he was giving sustenance to the hypocrites he derided. Whether he came to recognize himself as one of them, whether he ever came to see himself, in Frederick Brown's harsh words, as "the man who hides behind masks to avoid himself,"[6] we may never know. But one thing, at least, is certain: in *Diary of an Unknown,* we see him embarked down that path, and if it is true, as he says, that he tends "to go astray," that is only as it should be—it was a dark path, taken at a late age, and one that was wholly unfamiliar to him. In negotiating this path, Cocteau has bequeathed his readers a facet of his intriguing personality that has rarely, if ever, been so nakedly exposed to public scrutiny. This alone—disregarding the book's very conspicuous originality, its enormous compass of endeavor, and the beauty of its language—makes it an invaluable document for scholars and amateurs alike.

JESSE BROWNER

NOTES

1. Blanchard Bates, "Introduction" to the *Selected Essays* of Montaigne. New York: Random House, 1949.
2. Jean Cocteau, *Past Tense.* Translated by Richard Howard. New York: Harcourt, Brace, Jovanovich, 1987.

Introduction

3. Quoted in Francis Steegmuller, "In Search of Cocteau." *New York Times Book Review,* Oct. 25, 1970, p. 2.
4. Robert Phelps, *Professional Secrets*. New York: Farrar, Straus, Giroux, 1970.
5. Quoted in Francis Steegmuller, *Cocteau*. Boston: Atlantic-Little Brown, 1970.
6. Frederick Brown, *An Impersonation of Angels*. New York: Viking, 1968.

DEDICATION

My dear René Bertrand,

I was unaware of your existence, as one is unaware of the backstage of the universe which is your field of study.

You became my friend after hearing me on the radio. I had been saying that "time is a phenomenon of perspectives." That was a typical example of one of those seeds which we blindly sow, and which happens to fall on fertile ground.

While writing these notes, I have thought of you, of the pessimism of your book, *L'univers cette unité,* an optimistic pessimism, since you study our poor world while tending to your vines.

Allow me to remind you of the recent Einstein incident reported in the American press, which gave you so much pleasure.

The University of Pennsylvania receives a letter from a scholar, indicating his discovery of a serious mistake in Einstein's most recent calculations. The letter is shown to Einstein. He announces that the scholar is in earnest, and that if anyone is in a position to refute his work, he asks that it be done publicly. Professors and journalists are invited to the great conference hall of the University. A blackboard has been set up on the podium.

For four hours, the scholar covers the blackboard with impenetrable ciphers. Then he points to one of these ciphers, saying: "There is the mistake." Einstein steps up on the podium, considers the incriminating cipher at length, erases it, picks up the chalk, and replaces it with another.

His accuser hides his face in his hands, utters a strange, hoarse cry, and rushes from the room.

When Einstein was asked to explain the scene, he answered that it would take several years to understand it. Alone on the podium, the blackboard reared its Mona Lisa face. What am I saying? Its awful abstraction of a smile.

If one of us were to catch the other out, it would be you, and I would flee for my life. But I will not put you under the obligation of inflicting that shame upon me.

It remains true nonetheless that our attachments are of that sort, and that I have no more hope for the success of my notes than do you for your books. Certain truths do not bear saying. They disturb a smugness within us. They'd like forcibly to lift the wing under which man hides his head. An acceptable attitude if it hadn't gone too far, and if it weren't already too late to hide one's head after having so often re-peated: "Go ahead, frighten me." Furthermore, truth has a protean face which man can look at fearlessly, since he is unable to recognize it.

Accept this dedication as the simple homage paid by an invisible man to his colleague.

Jean Cocteau
February 1952, Saint-Jean-Cap-Ferrat.

PREAMBLE

It is not my pretension to build a factory of the invisible, but rather to follow the example of craftsmen in matters requiring a deeper culture than is mine.

I'd like to set up shop at my own front door, and try to gain an understanding, by hand, of that on which wisdom bases its craft.

Having at my disposal neither the tools nor the precepts that facilitate such study, I must resign myself merely to restuffing that chair in which the soul, rather than the body, customarily sits.

I have often taken such pleasure in watching the little sidewalk tradesmen, that my work may well please those who take the same pleasure in that sort of sideshow and merchandise as myself.

A man of science once told me that we are more in touch with the unknown when we are not swaddled in doctrine, and with good luck when we throw our chips haphazardly on the numbers instead of doubling our stake; that, by dint of counting and recounting its own legs, science was holding itself back, and that truancy was more likely to put us on the right track; that an entire pack of hounds has been known to lose the scent when some pug's nose led it straight to the quarry. In any case, a thousand pardons for seeking excuses for my ignorance and the permission to re-stuff my own chair.

It was Ingres' mediocre violin playing which gave us a formula so useful that we are forced to wonder how people ever got along without it.

"Several strings to one's bow" is not the same thing. And if Leonardo had been born after Ingres, it would surely have been said of him that he played several different violins like a virtuoso.

I have neither telescope nor microscope. Only a certain skill at splicing, and at choosing the supplest cane.

It is to the class of craftsmen that I pledge allegiance. Craftsmanship is no longer fashionable in our era of mass production. But it is representative of that singularity so threatened by the plural's onrushing tide.

P.S. I have noticed—and Montaigne explains it better than I—how the imagination becomes unfettered in the countryside and goes wandering blindly if it is not concentrated on a specific object. This diary, chapter by chapter, is nothing but the discipline of a mind on vacation, regrouping itself so as not to be lost in leisure.

ON
INVISIBILITY

---

*Capable of anything. Sometimes, suddenly, the question
arises: might masterpieces be nothing but alibis?*

ESSAI DE CRITIQUE INDIRECTE†

It seems to me that invisibility is the required provision of elegance. Elegance ceases to exist when it is noticed. Poetry, being elegance itself, cannot hope to achieve visibility. In that case, you ask me, of what use is it? Of no use. Who will see it? No one. Which does not prevent it from being an outrage to modesty, though its exhibitionism is squandered on the blind. It is enough for poetry to express a personal ethic, which can then break away in the form of a work. It insists on living its own life. It becomes the pretext for a thousand misunderstandings that go by the name of glory.

Glory is absurd, stemming as it does from the herding instinct. A crowd gathers around an accident, discusses it, reinvents it, worries at it until it has become something wholly different.

†Jean Cocteau, 1932. Throughout this edition, Cocteau's own footnotes are designated by a *. Translator's notes are designated by a †.

Beauty is always the result of an accident. Of a violent lapse between acquired habits and those yet to be acquired. It baffles and disgusts. It may even horrify. Once the new habit has been acquired, the accident ceases to be an accident. It becomes classical and loses its shock value. A work, therefore, is never perceived. It is received. If I am not mistaken, this was a remark made by Eugène Delacroix: "One is never perceived, one is received." It is a maxim frequently repeated by Matisse. Those who actually saw the accident hasten away, overwhelmed, unable to describe it. Those who did not see it are left to bear witness. This opportunity to make themselves seem important provides the medium through which they express their stupidity. The accident remains in the road, bloodied, petrified, awful in its solitude, a prey to gossip and police reports.

The inaccuracy of such gossip and such reports is not exclusively the result of distraction. It has more solid roots. It is closely related to the genesis of myth. Man seeks to escape himself in myth, and does so by any means at his disposal.* Drugs, alcohol, or lies. Unable to withdraw into himself, he disguises himself. Lies and inaccuracy give him a few moments of comfort, the trifling feeling of escape experienced at a masked ball. He distances himself from that which he feels and sees. He invents. He transfigures. He mythifies. He creates. He fancies himself an artist. He

*Lying is the only art form that the public sanctions and instinctively prefers to reality.   *Essai de critique indirecte*

imitates, in his small way, the painters he claims are mad.

Journalists know this, or at least sense it. The inaccuracies of the press, and the banner headlines by which they are trumpeted, are soothing draughts to this thirst for the unreal. Sadly, no authority presides in this case over the model's metamorphosis into a work of art. But it is this bland metamorphosis that demonstrates the need for myth. Accuracy is vexing to a crowd of would-be fantasizers. Hasn't our age coined the term "escapism," when in fact the only way to escape oneself is to allow oneself to be invaded?

It is for this reason that fantasy is detestable. People confuse it with poetry, whose modesty consists of masking its own equations. Its realism depicts a very strange reality, intrinsic to the poet who uncovers it and who is determined never to betray it.

Poetry is a religion without hope. The poet exhausts himself in its service, knowing that, in the long run, a masterpiece is nothing but the performance of a trained dog on very shaky ground.

Naturally, he consoles himself with the illusion that his work is grounded in some more concrete mystery. But this hope comes from the fact that every man is a night (harbors a night), that an artist's task is to bring that night into the light of day, and that this secular night provides a comforting extension of man's severe limitations. Man thereby becomes a sort of sleeping cripple, dreaming that he can walk.

Poetry is an ethic. By ethic I mean a secret code of behavior, a discipline constructed and conducted according to the capabilities of a man who rejects the falsifications of the categorical imperative.

This personal morality may appear to be immorality itself in the eyes of those who lie to themselves, or who live a life of confusion, in such a manner that, for them, a lie becomes the truth, and our truth becomes a lie.

It is in regard to this principle that I wrote that Genet is a moralist, and that "I am a lie that always tells the truth," a saying on which asses have grazed and frolicked with great relish. This saying was meant to imply that man is a social lie. The poet takes up arms against this social lie particularly when he upbraids its monadic truth and charges it with mendacity.

Nothing is more bitter than the defense which the plural puts up against the singular. Parrots of every feather squawk, "He's lying. He's a swindler," when a person devotes himself to never lying. Once, a young woman who was arguing with me cried out: "Your truth is not mine." I should hope not.

For that matter, how *could* I lie? In relation to what? To what purpose? By what right? I am on the one hand too lazy, and on the other too respectful of the inner orders that direct me, that compel me to overcome my laziness, and that don't waste their time catering to scandalmongers.

I have even reached the point where I am no longer aware of censure, being too engrossed in my ethic. (I wrote in *Le coq et l'arlequin*[1]: "We shelter an angel within us. We must be the guardians of that angel.") It is an ethic that I have perfected to the point of surrounding myself with friends who observe me with a steely gaze, and never let my slightest mistake go by unnoted. The sort of friends in whom goodness, grace, and virtue possess the kind of violence usually associated with spitefulness, foibles, and vice.

I call a work of art the sweat of this ethic.

Any work that is not the sweat of an ethic, any work not stemming from an exertion of the soul's will more strenuous than any physical labor, any work that is too visible (since the personal ethic and the works of art it engenders cannot be seen by those who live without an ethic, or who are content to follow a standardized code), any work that persuades too readily, will be but a decorative fantasy. It will please because it will not require the listener to subordinate his own personality to the personality of the speaker. It will allow the critics and those who defer to them to recognize it—and to recognize themselves in it—with a cursory glance. Yet beauty cannot be recognized with a cursory glance.

As it develops, this ethic will become a kind of insult. It will persuade only those who are able to abandon themselves to a greater force, and those who love more than they admire. It will accumulate neither subscribers nor admirers. It will only make friends.

When a primitive man experiences fear, he carves himself a god of fear, and asks that god to take away his fear. He fears this god born of his own fear. He expels his fear in the shape of an object, which becomes a work of art through the intensity of this fear, and an idol because the object, born of moral weakness, is transformed into a power that compels him to change. This is why a work of art, born of a personal ethic, breaks away from that ethic, often exploiting its powers of persuasion to opposite effect, even to the extent of altering those of the artist's feelings that gave birth to it.

Certain philosophers inquire into the question of whether the gods are named by men, or whether they inspire men to name them; in short, whether the poet creates, or whether he receives orders from a source higher than his own ministry.

This is the same old song about inspiration, which is actually nothing but expiration, since, while it is true that the poet receives orders, he receives them from a night which the centuries have nurtured within him, whither he cannot descend, which yearns for the light, and for which he is but the humble vehicle.

It is this vehicle that he will have to care for, to clean, to oil, to attend to, and to control tirelessly in order to make it fit for the unusual duties that will be required of it. And it is the control of this vehicle (which must never be allowed to slacken) that I call personal ethic, and to the demands of which it is essential to submit, particularly when everything points to the conclusion that this thankless obedience attracts nothing but scorn.

To renounce the implicit modesty of such an obedience would mean taking up one's own trumpet, substituting the ornamental for the implacable, considering oneself above one's own inner twilight, and, under the pretext of wishing to please, answering to someone else, instead of imposing our own inner gods upon that person and compelling him to believe in them.

Such modesty sometimes brings down the hatred of the incredulous upon us, accusations of false pride, artifice, and heresy, and may even lead us to be burnt in public at the stake.

No matter. We must not for one minute be distracted from a task that is all the more difficult for being inevitable, incomprehensible, and incapable of offering us the slightest hope.

Only a nation enamored of vainglory would place its hope in the sort of posthumous justice that the poet—who is a cynic in matters of earthly eternity, and whose only concern is to keep his balance on the high-wire from which his compatriots delight in trying to make him fall—could only find depressing.

It must be this balancing act above the void that allows us to be taken for acrobats, and the bringing to light of our secrets, a true feat of archaeology, that gets us mistaken for conjurers.

I have left Paris, where they are cultivating the art of Mexican torture. The victim is drenched in honey, after which he is left to be eaten by the ants.

It so happens that the ants devour each other, giving one the chance to take flight.

I have abandoned the streets of grey snow, and have come to the gardens of this Villa Santo Sospir, which I have covered in tattoos like a living person; it's a true haven, so well has the young woman who owns it managed to sequester its solitude.

The air is refreshing. The lemons are dropping onto the grass. But alas! Paris clings to the soul, and I drag its black thread behind me still. It will take time and patience for the glue to dry out, scab over, and flake off on its own. The iodine and salt will take care of that. Then, too, will I shed this coat of filthy calumny that covers me.

The regimen begins. Step by step, like the bath of Orestes, the soul's skin is cleansed once more.

I am without doubt the most unknown and the most famous of poets. This saddens me at times, because I am intimidated by celebrity and wish only to be loved. The sadness must stem from that mud in which we are steeped, and against which I struggle. When I think about it, however, I am able to deride my own sadness. And I believe that my visibility, built upon ridiculous legends, protects my invisibility, wraps it in a thick, glittering armor that is able to withstand the hardest of blows.

When people think they have wounded me, they have wounded a stranger whose acquaintance I have no desire to make, and when they stick pins into a wax effigy that represents me, the effigy bears so little likeness that the sorcery goes awry and fails to affect me. It is not that I boast of being beyond reach; yet a strange destiny has somehow managed to place beyond reach that vehicle that is me.

It used to be that artists were surrounded by a conspiracy of silence. Nowadays, the artist is surrounded by a conspiracy of noise. There is nothing that is not dissected and devalued. A dizzy self-destructiveness has swept through France. Like Nero, she kills herself crying: "What an artist dies with me!" She makes it a point of honor to destroy herself, and of pride to trample upon her pride. Her youth gathers in caverns and offers a legitimate resistance to the contempt in which it is held at all times, except for when it is sent off to do battle.

In the midst of such babeldom, the poet should be pleased to have built and lived his ethic in the solitude of an innocent who is deaf to the charges laid against him, not seeking to prove his innocence, amused by the crimes he is charged with, and accepting the penalty of death.

For this innocent understands that innocence is guilty by default, and that it is better to be accused of a real crime whose plea will be heard, than to be unjustly accused of imaginary crimes against unreality, against which reality has no recourse of self-defense.

Art consecrates the murder of a habit. The artist appoints himself the job of wringing its neck.

These confused times, for instance, find themselves taken in the painter's trap, as little by little we have developed the habit of comparing a painting with other paintings, instead of comparing a painting with its model. The result is that the intensity of the process that transforms a model into a work of art remains a dead letter. Only the shock of a novel similitude is felt, the similitude that non-figurative paintings are said by common consent to bear to each other, by the sole fact that they avoid the old kind of similitude; and these paintings reassure the public through a non-representationalism that it recognizes and believes to be a triumph over representationalism. While Picasso communicates the same intensity whether he chooses magnificently to deform the human face, or to render it as it actually is. Picasso is accorded this liberty because of the broadness of his scope, and because people accept the fact that he changes course in mid-stride; but he is the only one permitted to do so. This leads to the utterance of such phrases as that spoken to me over the telephone by a young man who had just come from seeing his latest canvases at Vallauris: "Astonishing paintings, figurative though they are."

Such a young man will never be as daring as the painter who tomorrow contradicts a hurricane with a calm sky, who resurrects the figurative through a hidden, subversive intensity, and through a rebellion against habits so entrenched that no painter can yet resolve himself to becoming the scapegoat of such an event. Should he dare to attempt it, he will undoubtedly be mistaken for a laggard, while he will actually be giving proof of transcendent heroism.

The ethic of this future victim will have to be strong, since his work will not reap the normal rewards of scandal, his scandal consisting precisely in not causing one.

I myself have known such solitude since I left the barrier that obstructed my path. (I had been running up and down the wrong track for some time.) This leap was all the more a fall amongst colleagues who considered it at first as a climb up the wall of a private estate, guarded by attack dogs.*

My isolation has endured, and I have come to terms with it. In each case, a work of mine sets its face

---

*Having spent a good deal of time with Marcel Proust, at a time when I was no older than he had been when he wrote *Les plaisirs et les jours*,[2] I accepted as quite natural that he should treat me as if I had already crossed this threshold and set off on that painful road that I should one day take, and on which he himself was travelling. Surely Proust, who was unparalleled in fathoming the architecture of a life, knew far more than I about this future entirely concealed from me, particularly as I then considered myself in top form, whereas I could later look back and see my life as the series of grave errors it had been. The explanation of his indulgence towards me can be found on page 122 of *A l'ombre des jeunes filles en fleur*.[3]

This is why so many of Proust's letters seemed incomprehensible to me, bathed as they were in a future that was clear to him and could not possibly be so to me.

His was a dark room, in which he developed photographic plates, at a time in human life when the future and the past stumble over one another. I profited from this development, and I sometimes regret having known Marcel at an age when, despite my respect for his work, I was not yet worthy to appreciate it.

against that which it betokens. It is suspect from birth.*

The diversity of my undertakings has saved me from becoming a habit. This diversity has confounded inattentive minds by following methods that are extreme while appearing not to be. It made people believe that I was exploiting these methods without understanding them, while I was countering such belief in my writing, my theater, and my film for an elite that was both blind and deaf. For the masses, in losing their individuality, never reject individualism and willingly allow themselves to be pervaded by an idea in a theater that would disgust them in private. Untainted by snobbery, they have almost always sounded me out. This, of course, in the realm of the theater and the cinema. A paying audience does not prejudge, it thrills elbow to elbow, opens itself wide, and does not distance itself from the show like an invited observer, who wears a wet suit proof against all charm.

So it was that I was seen as erratic, dispersed, when in fact I was positioning and repositioning my lantern, in order to illuminate from many angles the different aspects of the solitude of beings and of free will.

Free will is the product of a limitless coexistence of opposites that join, blend with one another,

*I was trained in this school of thought by Raymond Radiguet, when he was fifteen years old. He told me: "You must write novels *just like everyone else's*. You must contradict the avant-garde. It's the only truly execrable stance you can take these days. The only stance of any worth."

and form a single entity. Man believes himself free to choose because he wavers between choices that are actually all of a whole, but amongst which he makes distinctions in his own fashion. Shall I take the right or the left? It comes to the same thing. The one road and the other take up their positions and slyly pretend to contradict each other. This is why man is constantly questioning himself, wondering whether he's right or wrong, whereas he's neither right nor wrong and, without being free, he seems to choose one of many mutually opposing threads whose tangled skein forms his immutable yet apparently progressive weave.

I've noticed that my invisibility is in danger of becoming visible at a distance, in those countries where I am judged through the medium of works that may even be poorly translated, whereas in my own country I am judged through a persona that is counterfeited for me.

But all this is rather vague. In all honesty, I think that the visible does play a role in the interest I provoke abroad, and that my fake personality does intrigue. I notice this when I am travelling and people are disconcerted by my appearance, so strongly does it contradict the advertised model.

In the final analysis, I should probably give up trying to unravel this mess. For it is not a simple thing to set in motion the persona-vehicle and the work-vehicle, and works tend to pursue that wild freedom of all offspring, dreaming only of exploring the world and of selling themselves to it.

A thousand dangers threaten the birth of a work of art, both from within and from without. An individual is a night constellated by cells that float in a sustaining magnetic fluid. They revolve in the same manner as the dead or living cells that we call stars, whose great separating distances are repeated within us.

It would seem that cancer comes from a disorder in our magnetic fluid (in our sky) and from a flaw in the astral machinery sustained by that fluid.

A magnet arranges iron filings in a flawless design, similar to frost, to the insect's markings, to a flower. Introduce a foreign body (a hairpin, for instance) between one pole of the magnet and the filings, and the design rearranges itself—*not in the spot corresponding to the position of the pin,* but as a localized anarchy in the filings, which pile up chaotically on a dead spot.

Where shall we find such a pin within ourselves? Our inner design, alas, is too changeable, too complex, too subtle. If our thumb were not composed of interstellar spaces, it would weigh several thousand tons. This makes research a delicate business. The phenomenon (since the universal mechanism is a unity— a simple one at that—and its matter consists of a kaleidoscopic triangle)* will therefore be analogous to human experience wherein the slightest flaw can provoke an anarchy of ideas, can disorganize the re-

---

*It may well be that the invention of the kaleidoscope was the discovery of a great secret. For its infinite combinations stem from three apparently unrelated elements. A rotation. Pieces of glass. A mirror. (The mirror coordinates the two elements of rotation and glass.)

volving atomic structure which a work of art should be.

The most negligible foreign body on either pole of the magnet is carcinogenic to our work.

Fortunately, our organism goes on the defensive as soon as the mind begins to wander. It sometimes helps us to ward off the evil which would otherwise eat away at our work and destroy its flesh. I related in *Opium*[4] how my novel *Les enfants terribles*[5] left me high and dry because I allowed myself to be "determined to write it."

It often happens that a needle, going unnoticed at first, induces through a kind of cellular anarchy a veritable disease of circumstances in the fate of a written work, and that books betray their author's intentions.

The least initiative, other than the unforeseeable occlusions of our fluid, can upset the dark forces that require us to be passive, yet also actively attentive in ensuring them a form in human scale. What control must we exercise, then, in that half-sleep between the conscious and the unconscious, a control which must be neither too strong, thereby denying the work its transcendence, nor too weak, thereby leaving it in the dream state and depriving it of its human contact.

Man is a cripple. By this I mean that he is limited by finite dimensions that prevent him from understanding the infinite, where dimensions do not exist.

It will be through his shame of this debility, and

the yearning to overcome it, rather than through science, that he will be able to conceive the inconceivable. Or at least to admit that the machinery in which he occupies a very humble place was not designed with him in mind.*

He is even beginning to recognize that eternity could not *have been* nor *will be,* that it is somehow immutable, that it *is,* that it is enough for it *to be,* that minutes are equal to centuries and centuries to minutes, and that there are neither minutes nor centuries, but a pulsing, teeming, terrifying immobility against which his pride bridles, to the point where he has come to believe his to be the sole dwelling place, and himself the king of it.

Recant though he may, he continues to dismiss the thought that his dwelling place might be a speck of dust in the Milky Way. He is revolted by the painful certainty that the cells within us are as distant from each other and as ignorant of our existence as are the stars. And he finds it unpleasant to speculate that he may be living on the yet-warm crust of an ember flung off by the sun, that this ember is cooling down very quickly, and that it is only an illusory perspective that stretches this rapid process into the length of several billion centuries. (Of this kind of perspective I will speak later.)

---

*According to Calligaris, a certain acupunctural technique (for instance, cold applied against the posterior surface of the right leg, about 1 inch within the axial line, and on a plane that passes about 2 inches beneath the mid-section of that leg) can unleash certain reflexes, enabling us to catch time-space red-handed in its lie, and giving the subject the illusion of having become a visionary. The things that he predicted were later noticed to have taken place.

It is his struggle against a certain forgivable pessimism that has caused him to make up games to distract himself on his voyage from birth to death.

Even if he is a believer (and but little worthy of rewards or of punishments out of all proportion to his merit), his principal remedy against pessimism is to believe that at the terminal stage of his voyage awaits apotheosis or hell-fire, which he still prefers to the notion of being nothing at all.

In order to overcome his uneasiness in being bound to the incomprehensible, he tries to make it comprehensible and, for instance, to ascribe to patriotism the hecatombs for which he claims responsibility, and which are nothing but a noisome tendency of the earth to shake off its fleas and relieve its itchings.

This is so true that science, which with one hand cures plagues, invents with the other destructive weaponry that nature compels man to use, asking not that her victims be saved but that she be helped to create more of them, until she has achieved a balance in her body of human livestock, just as she achieves a balance in her bodies of water.

Luckily, protracted seem the brief respites between the earth's shruggings in which, with a frown, it overturns its continental morphology, alters its profiles, the depths of its seas, and the height of its mountains.

Nature is naïve. Maurice Maeterlinck relates how a very tall plant would make parachutes for its seed, and how it persists in doing so now that it has degenerated into a dwarf species. I have seen on the Cap Nègre a wild orange tree which, having been domesticated, reverted to the wild state, arming itself with long thorns on the small portion of its surface that was threatened by the shadow of a palm tree. The least amount of sunshine suffices to trick the sap into foolishly exposing itself to the first frost. And so it goes.

Our mistake must have been in seeking to understand what was happening on every floor of the house.

To this pre-Adamic curiosity we owe progress, which is but a stubborn persistence in a gratuitous error, well-suited to nurturing this error to its final consequences.

It is surprising that art can survive on a planet hell-bent on destroying itself, and that its manifestations, which should pass for expendable luxuries (and which, on that account, certain mystics would like to see abolished) can maintain their prerogatives, can interest so many people, and have become currencies of exchange. The monied circles having come to see that thought can be sold, gangs have set themselves up to reap its profit. Some think in terms of works, others of their exploitation. As a result, money has become more abstract than spirit. Rarely does spirit get the upper hand.

These are times in which swindlers juggle with a low form of invisibility known as fraud.

"The Treasury is ripping me off. I'll rip off the

Treasury." Such is the intermediary's reasoning. His imagination outruns that of the artist he is exploiting. He becomes a great artist in his own right. He maintains the balance that rules only through imbalance and trade-offs. Were he not to commit fraud, the blood of a hoarding nation would clot and coagulate.

Nature gives orders. Men disobey her. She manages to bring them to heel by using their own trick of forging inequalities in an otherwise balanced system. She is as sly as a savage beast. Equally partial, it would seem, to life and to death, she thinks only of her own belly and of pursuing an invisible task whose visibility gives proof of her complete indifference to individual suffering. Individuals don't see it that way. They like to see themselves as responsible and sensitive. For instance, when an old woman is trapped beneath the rubble, when a submarine sinks, when a spelunker plunges into a crevasse, when a plane is lost in the mountains. When disaster assumes a human face. *When it looks like one of them*. But when disaster adds noughts to a number, when it is anonymous, when it is deindividualized, individuals lose interest—unless they become concerned that the disaster should overflow the banks of anonymity to which they have relegated it, and threaten their own fate.

The same goes for the pilot who bombs a world reduced to a size that requires an imaginative effort to be reconstituted in human scale. The inhumanity of those who drop bombs stems from the fact that they are no longer able to conceive of that scale, and believe themselves to be bombing some plaything in which individuals could not possibly live or travel.

It seems that the human imagination of these pilots is switched on at the very moment when they are readying themselves to destroy inhumanly. An example is provided in the book written by the pilots who bombed Hiroshima and Nagasaki.* But they too were acting under orders, orders that reflected other orders drawn from the invisible and which minister to the machinery that is my concern, a machinery that shuffles the deck of responsibility.

Only, responsibility compels man, over and above his own arrogance, to hold himself responsible and to minister to invisibility while yet seeking to exonerate himself. For if he offers to ban nuclear weapons, it is not with the aim of making war impossible, it is with the aim of making it possible. Autophagous nature whispers this advice in his ear until he is convinced that the atomic bomb will alleviate his misfortunes.

Along these lines, one can imagine the danger of an unstable alliance between our secret orders and the factitious orders that are imposed upon them. Nature herself, obtuse in her own way, loses herself amongst these twisting directives that lead to pitfalls, whence she picks herself up from amongst our corpses and lopes off on her stubborn, bestial way.

Astrologists do not fail to ascribe these pitfalls to the influence of the stars, whereas they are ascribable

*The bombardiers were named M. Millerand and A. Spitzer. Their machine, *The Great Artist*.

to the fact that we contain stars, that we are a nebula, and that their calculations would be just as valid if they swapped their telescopes for microscopes and pointed them within themselves, where perhaps they might discover the astrological indices of our slavery.

A relative slavery, to which perforce I will return.

We are deeply involved with ourselves. It is too easy to take advantage of this outlet, and too easy to deny responsibility for actions that hinder those expected of us (that disoblige our inner twilight).

Which false notes are mine in the symphony of recriminations that blares about my ears? Have I given no cause for complaint?

The time has come to descend from the heights. Since I am writing for friends, perhaps I owe it to them to look myself in the face, to go from the role of accuser to the role of accused. Perhaps it is only fair that I accuse myself.

Of what? Of countless mistakes that have brought down the storm upon me, not only from without, but also from within. Countless little mistakes that are disastrous when one has decided not to commit any, and to respect one's ethic.

I have slipped often on the steep slope of visibility, and grabbed at the ledge it extended to me. I should have been tough. I was weak. I thought myself beyond reach. I said to myself: "My armor protects me," and I didn't bother to repair its cracks. They became wide breaches open to the enemy.

Instead of understanding that the audience is made up of four-legged animals who flap their front paws one against the other, I allowed myself to be seduced by applause. I kept telling myself that it made up for the conspirators. I committed the crime of letting myself be hurt by the insults and of considering the praise as my due.

I took my good health for granted, so I did not save my strength. But when I fell ill, I found it unbearable and railed against my fate.

All of this has very little in common with a rigid ethic. The disgust I felt at this realization threw me into a pessimism which I flaunted before my friends. I demoralized them. I was determined to convince them of their powerlessness to cure me. It was a hateful labor, to which I devoted myself until the anger of the invisible was unleashed and made me ashamed. And all this from one minute to the next, in manner such that my friends began to wonder if I were tormenting them gratuitously.

On this sunny coast where I am resting, I have thrown a shadow about myself. Since I have started splashing the ink around I have found some peace, except at those times when I seek to discover whether the ink has come from my inkwell or from my veins. At such times pessimism wins out. Optimism recedes. I attribute the return of my pessimism to the liberties I attempt to take in my work. I sadden my household. Reproaching myself for it, I grow tense instead of relaxing, which would be the least of generous compulsions.

The mail arrives. It's a package from town. A hundred letters tumble out, bearing stamps of all nations. My pessimism knows no bounds. What, must I read all these letters and answer them? I have never had a secretary. I do my own writing and open my own front door. People come in. Is it not some morbid desire to please that drives me? Is it not the fear of being isolated? That's when the struggle begins between the anxiety of wasting my time and the guilt of leaving the letters in sufferance, in the literal sense of the word.

If I reply, there will be a reply to my replying. If I stop replying, reproof. If I avoid replying altogether, grievance. I know for a certainty that my heart will win out. I am fooling myself, because it is weakness that wins out over the true duties of my heart. Do I not owe myself to my loved ones? This time is stolen from them. And I am stealing it, too, from the forces whose handservant I am. They revenge themselves by having me take up responsibilities marginal to my commitment.

It's all a fine mess. First, I accuse myself of dabbling with powers that ought to be hidden, of speaking unwisely, of sousing myself on monologues, of giving myself over to endless, distracting chitchat.

Then, I take up my own defense: isn't this orgy of words the only way to whip myself into the frenzy of writing, since I have no real intelligence of my own? If I don't get the machinery in motion, I begin to vegetate, to think of nothing. This void terrifies me and flings me into the arms of discourse.

After which I go to bed. Instead of retreating into a book, I retreat into sleep, into those intensely complex dreams I have, dreams of such realistic unreality that I sometimes confuse them with reality.

All of this helps to blur the distinctions between

responsibility and irresponsibility, between the visible and the invisible.

I get to the point of wondering whether I am not quite simply stupid, whether this intelligence that I am supposed to have (and for which I am reproached) is not some mirage of unknown provenance.

From intuition to intuition, from obedience to obedience, from disobedience to disobedience, from crisis of fortitude to crisis of fortitude, from crisis of lassitude to crisis of lassitude, from blunder to blunder, from sleight to sleight, I gracefully pick myself up as I fall down my stairs, in a daze, a cipher to others and to myself, like those princes who march up and down have learned to sleep with their eyes open.

Have I confused righteousness with the kind of blind obedience that binds us ineffably to our weaknesses? Have I led my ethic up a blind path, a dead end up which intelligence refuses to follow? Have I run my ship aground with my claim that one *should* sail badly? Am I shipwrecked on a desert island? Do people refuse to see me, or do my signals go unseen?

I am not a child, but very nearly. My childhood is endless. This is what makes people think that I remain youthful, while youth and childhood are not at all the same thing. Picasso said: "It takes a very long time to grow young." Youth chases off our childhood. In the end, childhood reclaims its rights.

My mother died in childhood. But she was not beaten down by childhood. She was a vivacious old child. She was able to recognize me, but *her* childhood

placed me in *mine,* while our two childhoods remained incongruously relative to one another. An old
little girl, set down amidst her little girl's occupations,
questioned an old little boy about his high school,
charging him to behave himself at school the next day.

This long childhood, passing itself off as
adulthood, may well come to me from my mother
(whom I resemble) and be the source of all my misfortunes. It could be that the invisible takes advantage of
it. No doubt, I owe it certain discoveries generally
reserved for children, in whom a sense of the
ridiculous does not exist. The sayings attributed to
them are close to the dissociations made by poets, and
I would be proud to have said some of them myself.

But no one cares to acknowledge the mixture of
childhood and old age within us, except in the guise of
senility. I am of such clay nonetheless. People sometimes scold and tease me, without realizing that they
are treating me the way parents treat their children.

They've got me by the short hairs, as they say. It's
not enough to accuse my goat of having eaten my
cabbage; they then have to accuse my cabbage of
having poisoned my goat.

Here is man, an unwieldy vehicle to operate. It is
quite natural that this man-vehicle should irritate that
night seeking to take shape, and which I impede
through sheer idiocy.

Even here, beneath the Nice sunshine—which
sometimes seems black to me, depending on whether
I lean to the right or to the left—I become once again
the pessimist-optimist that I have always been.

I have to wonder if I could possibly be otherwise,

and if the difficulties I have in being, the mistakes that hinder my development, aren't actually my process of development itself, and the regret of not having a different one. It is a fate as inescapable as my body. Thence come those fits of pessimism and optimism whose conjunction shatters me. The systole and diastole of the universal rhythm.

And this prompts us to mourn deaths and to rejoice at births, when our true condition is not to be at all.

Our pessimism grows from this void, this non-being. Our optimism, from a suggestive wisdom that we take advantage of the hiatus offered by this void, that we take advantage without seeking an answer to the riddle in which man can never have the final word, that our heavenly system is no more durable than our inner heavens, that duration is a myth, that the void is not empty, that we are hoodwinked by eternity into perceiving a passage of time when in fact the entirety of time and space explodes, statically, far from any concept of time and space.

In the final analysis, man is a swaggerer, and no one would dare to assert that our entire system is perhaps contained within a pinhead or the body of an individual. Only Renan† has dared to do so, in a fairly gloomy little sentence: "It may be that the truth was sad."

†Joseph-Ernest Renan, 1823–1892. French philosopher and historian. His most famous work is a series of Christian histories, *Histoire des origines du christianisme*.

Art should follow the example of crime. The glamor that surrounds the criminal would evaporate were he to become visible, or to fall down on the job. His glory is contingent on loss, unless he robs or kills for the very glory of losing, and is unable to confess his crime without the apotheosis of punishment.

The enigma of the visible and the invisible retains its enigmatic elegance. It cannot be resolved in a world fascinated by factuality and possessed of no other resource. It is not well-disposed toward commerce. It follows a rhythm contradictory to that of society, since the social rhythm is merely an ancient rhythm all primped up. Never has speed been so slow. Mme. de Stael was able to travel faster from one end of Europe to the other than we are, and it took Caesar just eight days to conquer the Gauls.

It is not easy for me to write this chapter. Our French language being comprised of several different languages, we are sometimes as misunderstood in France as if we were writing in a foreign language. I know people who balk at reading Montaigne and are confused by him, whereas he speaks to me in a language in which every word has meaning. On the other hand, I sometimes have to reread a newspaper article in order to grasp its meaning. I have but few words at my disposal. I compound them until they squeeze out some sort of meaning. But the forces that compel me to write are impatient. They hustle me along, which does nothing to ease the burden of my compulsion.

Furthermore, I avoid the terminology of scholars and philosophers, which makes up yet another foreign language that is hard for my intended audience to follow. It is true that those for whom I am writing have their own language that is not my own. The invisible stands to gain from this fact; so does pessimism. For one might wish to participate in the dance of joy, only to find oneself shut out.

If this book should fall into the hands of some conscientious young man, I advise him to apply his brakes, to reread a sentence too quickly read, to think of the pains I have taken to intercept those frequencies that scorn the confused environment in which he flounders and which he seeks to escape. I ask him to fly from the plurality that rebuffs him, toward the absolute tendered by his own night. Unlike Gide, I do not tell him: "Go, leave your family and your home." I tell him: "Stay and seek refuge in your own inner twilight. Inspect it. Drag it into broad daylight."

I do not ask him to take an interest in my frequencies, but to learn through the vehicle that emits them to build one of his own, one that will be suitable to him and capable of emitting his own frequencies. For a well-structured vehicle is what is lacking in youthful vigor. That much is apparent in the countless manuscripts that are sent to me.

One should not confuse the night of which I speak with that into which Freud urged his patients to descend. Freud was the plunderer of poor tenements.

He removed a few mediocre pieces of furniture and some erotic photographs. He never consecrated the abnormal with transcendental value. He never broached the great disorders. He provided a confessional to buttonholers.

A lady in New York spoke to me of her affection for Marlene Dietrich, and as I was praising Marlene's soul, she interrupted: *"It's not that, but she listens to me."* The ever-patient Marlene would listen to her in a city that abides neither complaint nor pity, and blocks its ears in instinctive self-defense against the contagious sickness of confidentiality. The lady had relieved herself on the cheap. Elsewhere, preying on boors, psychoanalysts take on that task. I commend them for taking payment through the nose.

Freud's key to dreams is extremely naïve. It baptizes the simple as complexity. His sexual obsession seduced a timid society for which sex was pivotal. Research in America has shown that the plural remains plural even when it has singularized itself and confessed its self-fabricated vices. It is the same foolishness that governs both the confession of vice and the display of virtue.

Freud is readily accessible. His hell (his purgatory) is measured in whole numbers. Contrary to our study, he is seeking only visibility.

The night with which I am concerned is different. It is a treasure trove. Neither a doctor nor a neurosis can open it—just a little daring and an "open sesame." It becomes dangerous if its treasures make us forget the password.

It is from this trove, from this untapped source of

luxury, from this *parlor beneath the lake,* that all great souls enrich themselves.

As one might guess, sexuality is not without its role in all this. Da Vinci and Michelangelo prove it, but their secrets have little in common with Freud's little redecorating schemes.*

The vulture incorporated in the folds of the Virgin's skirt in the painting by Leonardo, like the bag of acorns under the arm of the young man in the Sistine chapel, are examples of the many kinds of hide-and-seek once played by the masters. During the Renaissance, these did not bear reference to psychological disorders, but to a conniving will to outsmart the dictatorial Church police. These are quite significant pranks, in their own way. They reveal more of the protracted childhood of painters than of fixation. They speak more to friends than to analysts, and bear no more Freudian consequence than those microscopic students' signatures discovered in the ears and nostrils of Rubens' women.

As for the Oedipus complex, Freud would nearly coincide with our line of thought (the human night enticing us into one trap under the pretext of avoiding another), had Sophocles not believed in destiny. The gods play at devising a horrendous prank of which Oedipus is the victim.

I complicated this horrendous prank in *La ma-*

---

*The old sorcerer's trial (as Nietzsche would say), at which Emile Ludwig plays the part of Attorney General, indicts neither the discoveries of Dr. Breuer, nor the progress made by psychoanalysts and psychiatrists. They are no longer looking for their own illness in their patients. They are curing them.

chine infernale,[6] by making of Oedipus' triumph over the Sphinx a false triumph born of his pridefulness and of the weakness of the Sphinx, a half-god, half-female beast who gives him the answer to the riddle so as to spare him death. The Sphinx behaves as will the princess in my film *Orphée,*[7] when she believes herself condemned for the crime of free will. The Sphinx, intermediary between gods and men, is manipulated by the gods who allow it to think itself free, and who intimate that Oedipus should be saved, only so that he might be more thoroughly damned.

It is precisely through the Sphinx's treachery that I underline just how far is Oedipus from the center of the drama in the Greek conception, which I develop in *Orphée*. The gods spare Orpheus his death in order to render him immortal and blind, *and so as to deprive him of his muse*.

Freud's mistake was to have demeaned our night by turning it into a warehouse, to have opened it up though it is bottomless and impenetrable.

I have often been reprimanded for devoting so little space to nature in my works. This is because, first of all, I am more attracted by phenomena than by their results, and am primarily struck by the supernatural in nature. Secondly, others have done it better than I could ever hope to do, and it would be presumptuous to attempt to outdo Mme. Colette. On a wing or a petal, a wasp or a tiger, it is the secret of their markings that drives me to write. I am more fascinated by the underside than by the upside. It is a penchant that compels me to take great pleasure in things without trying to communicate my pleasure.

Each of us owes it to himself to remain within his own bounds and not to infringe on those of others. My own are found in a tendency to be satisfied only when vacuity offers me the illusion of a laden table.

That is the entire rationale behind this diary, in which neither the picturesque, nor science, nor philosophy, nor psychology are able to insinuate themselves.

It is thus seated between two chairs that I re-upholster the third, that phantom chair of which I spoke in my preamble.

P.S. The taste for responsibility. Very strong in a certain kind of childhood beset by family contempt. This childhood accuses itself of actions of which it is innocent (which remains to be seen, its responsibility quite possibly being unconscious).

It is not rare that children accept the blame for the phenomena that occur in a haunted house. Nor is it rare that these phenomena are characterized by the child's pleasure in surprise, which would explain their childish nature. Some power must escape from them, wreak its havoc, and then somehow induce them to confess to family and police that of which they believe themselves innocent. They want to share in both the visible and the invisible.

But the night of these children is still slumbering. Ours is active. It can conceive veritable tumors, monstrous growths. It can impregnate us with creatures that require exorcism, as the following chapter will demonstrate.

THE BIRTH OF A POEM

But the angel who grinds his face into the dust is himself.

SARTRE. SAINT GENET

I have just been pulled apart by several horses, the guinea pig in one of those Ravaillac-style quarterings by which we are exposed to the struggle between the forces for which we serve as battlefield. Having decided to make a study of the birth of one of my poems, *L'ange Heurtebise,* which, it seemed to me, was an apt depiction of the relationship between the visible and the invisible, the conscious and the unconscious, I found myself unable to write. The words dried up, jostled and entrammeled one another, piled up and ran riot in the manner of diseased tissue. They took up positions beneath my pen which prevented them from connecting and forming sentences. I stubbornly persisted, putting the blame on that sham clearsightedness that I try to set against my night. I reached the point of believing that I would never be free, or that age had rusted my vehicle, which would be worse still, since free or not, I envisioned myself incapable of aspiring to any work whatsoever. I erased, tore up, started over. Each time I ran up against the same brick wall. Each time I encountered the same obstacle.

I was about to give up, when I came across my book *Opium*, lying on a table. I opened it at random (if I dare use such an expression) and read a paragraph that elucidated my impotence. My memory had gone wrong, interpolating dates, overwinding the clockwork, jamming the mechanism. A deeper memory had been rebelling without my knowledge, and was resisting my mistakes.

A false perspective had me place one event before another, when it had in fact occurred later. In this way do our past actions telescope as they retreat in time, and their orchestration is thwarted by a false note, a false testimony given by one who pleads in his own defense.

Before my poem *L'ange Heurtebise,* the symbol "angel" bore as yet no relation in my work to any particular religious imagery, even when the Greek El Greco repudiated it, giving it an unwonted significance, and drawing upon himself the wrath of the Spanish Inquisition.

Much closer would be that which was seen by the crewmen of superfortress no. 42.7353, after they had dropped the first atomic bomb. They speak of a purple light and of a tower of indescribable hues. They want for words. The spectacle of the phenomenon remains locked up within them.

On the Birth of a Poem

The similarity between the words *angel* and *angle,* in which the word angel becomes angle by the addition of an *l* (or wing),† is a happenstance of the French language, if one can speak of happenstance in such matters. But I knew that the similarity is no quirk in Hebrew, in which the words for angel and angle are synonymous with one another.††

In the Bible, the fall of the angels symbolizes the fall of angles, in other words the entirely human creation of a conventional sphere. Emptied of its geometrical soul, made up of a tangle of hypotenuses and right angles, the sphere is no longer based on the points that guaranteed its radiance.

I knew, too, that it is incumbent upon us to preclude the fall of our geometrical soul, and that the loss of our angles or of our angels poses a threat to those individuals too anchored to the earth.

There is no passage in Genesis relating to the fall of the angels. These fabulous, disquieting creatures impregnated the daughters of men, who gave birth to giants. As a result, the distinction between giants and angels is confused in the Jewish imagination. Gustave Doré depicts marvelously that avalanche of bodies choking up the depths of desolated ravines with their inverted musculatures.

†Fr. *ange* = angel; Fr. *angle* = angle. The word *wing* refers to an untranslatable pun, the letter *l* in French being homonymous with the word *aile,* meaning wing.

††Cocteau is in error here. The Hebrew words for "angel" and "angle" have no etymological roots in common.

Whence came visibility in the notion of angels, the human shape taken by these inhumans? Surely, from man's need to explain certain forces, to overcome an abstract presence, to embody it somewhat in our own image, that it might be less frightening.

The phenomena of nature—lightning, eclipses, floods—would seem less inscrutable at the hands of some perceptible host, acting on God's orders.

In bearing human features, the lineaments of this host would lose that vagueness against which the mind revolts, that nameless quality that terrifies children and makes them leap breathlessly for the nearest lamp.

It is in this climate—though without the apocalyptic shadow—that the Greek gods were born. Each one legitimated a vice or magnified a virtue. They came and went between earth and heaven, between Olympus and Athens, as between the floors of a building. They reassured. Angels, on the other hand, were to be fear incarnate.

Graceful monsters, cruel, dreadfully masculine and androgynous—such was the notion I held of angels, of *flying angles,* before I discovered that their invisibility could be captured in a poem and made visible, *without running the risk of being seen.*

I had originally intended my play *Orphée* to be a story about the Virgin and Joseph, about the backbiting at their expense that was instigated by the angel (a carpenter's assistant), the malevolence of Nazareth confronted by an unaccountable pregnancy, and the necessity of the couple's flight occasioned by the village's spite.

The plot lent itself to so many misapprehensions that I was forced to abandon it. In its place I used the Orphic theme, in which the unaccountable birth of poems would replace that of the Holy Infant.

The angel was to have a part in it, in the guise of a glazier. But I was not to write the act until much later, at the Hotel Welcome in Villefranche, when I was free once more to disguise the angel in a blue tunic, with glass wings on his back. Several years later, he was no longer an angel and had become a nondescript young dead man, the princess' driver, in my film. (Which is why journalists make the mistake of calling him an angel.)

If I run ahead of myself, it is only in order to make it quite clear that the character of the angel lived platonically within me and gave me no cause for un-easiness before the poem, and that once I had finished the poem I considered him to be harmless. I kept only his name in the play and in the film. Having become a poem, he was but little concerned over whether or not I gave him any thought.

Here is the passage from *Opium* that shed light on my impotence to write this chapter. It dates from 1928. I had placed it in 1930.

> One day, on my way to visit Picasso in rue La Boétie, I felt that something terrible and eternal was growing within and next to me in the elevator. A voice called out to me: "My name is on the plate," a jolt brought me to my senses, and I read on the

brass plate affixed to the hand lever: HEURTEBISE
ELEVATORS.

I recall that, later, Picasso and I spoke about
miracles. Picasso said that everything is a miracle,
that it's a miracle that we don't dissolve in our baths.

In retrospect, I see how deeply that sentence
influenced me. It sums up the style of a play in which
miracles must appear not to be miraculous, must re-
flect both comedy and tragedy, must fascinate in the
way that the adult world fascinates children.

I thought no more about the incident in the elevator. Then, suddenly, everything changed. The outline of my projected play became blurred. At night, I
would fall asleep then awaken abruptly, unable to go
back to sleep. During the day, I floundered and stum-
bled in a quagmire of daydreams. This agitation became atrocious. The angel had taken up residence
within me without my knowing it, and it had taken
this name Heurtebise, with which I became ever more
obsessed, to make me aware of it.

By dint of continually hearing this name, of hearing it without hearing it, of hearing its shape, in a
manner of speaking, in some region where man cannot stop his ears, by dint of hearing this name clam-
orously shouted out in silence, by dint of being
hounded by this name, I was brought back to the voice
in the elevator—"My name is on the plaque"—and I
gave a name to this angel rebelling against my
foolishness, since it had already named itself and I
had yet to do so. In giving it a name, I hoped that it
would leave me alone. I was sadly mistaken. The

mythical creature became unbearable. It grew burdensome, spread its wings, thrashed about, kicked like a baby in its mother's womb. I could confide in no one. I was compelled to bear the torture. For the angel tormented me, to the point where I began using opium, hoping to pacify it through trickery. But the trick displeased it, and I was made to pay dearly for it.

Today, on this temperate coast, it is hard for me to relive the details of that time and its wretched symptoms. We have a talent for forgetting the ills that protect us. Only our deepest memory keeps vigil, which is why we remember a childhood gesture better than a recently accomplished action. By arousing this double memory, I can put myself in a state that is inconceivable to those who do not practice our ministry. And slyly, in open disobedience to this ministry, I who boasted of being free find myself back in frock, my pen racing, no longer paralyzed. I am staying on the rue d'Anjou. My mother is alive. I can trace my own anxieties in her face. She does not question me. She suffers. I suffer. And the angel scoffs. It carries on demonically. "Get yourself exorcised," people tell me. "There's a devil in you." No, it's an angel. A creature that is looking for a form, one of those creatures who seem by some rule to be denied access to our kingdom, to which they are drawn by curiosity and in which they would use any means available to get a foothold.

The angel couldn't have cared less about my rebellion. I was only its vehicle, and it treated me like one. It made ready for its departure. My crises came more and more frequently, becoming one single crisis akin to labor pains. But it was a monstrous birth, one which would benefit neither from the maternal instinct nor from the closeness it engenders. Imagine a parthenogenesis, a couple formed of one body that gives birth. At last, after a night in which I had contemplated suicide, the delivery took place, on the rue d'Anjou. It lasted seven days, during which the character's gall exceeded all bounds, compelling me to write against my will.

That which leaked out of me, inscribing itself as on the pages of a type of album, had to do neither with Mallarmé's frost nor Rimbaud's golden lightning, nor with automatic writing, nor with anything that I had ever known. It moved about like chess pieces, reorganized itself as if the Alexandrine rhythm had broken itself down and reconstituted itself according to its own lights. As if it were dissecting a temple, it measured its columns, its arcades, its cornices, its scrolls, and its architraves, made errors and started its calculations again from scratch. It frosted an opaque window, interwove lines, right-angle triangles, hypotenuses, diameters. It added, multiplied, divided. It violated my intimate memories in order to humanize its equations. It grabbed me by the scruff of my neck, bent me over the page, and I was compelled to wait on the insufferable invader's hesitations and recoveries, to break myself in the service it demanded of my ink, through which it dripped into a poem. I was buoyed by the hope that this would rid me of its burdensome presence, that it would become another, extrinsic to me. I had no interest in its intentions. The important thing was my passive submission to its metamorphosis. It would be too much to call me an assistant, for it seemed to expect no assistance of me, and offered me only its contempt. There was no longer any question of sleeping, nor of living. There was only its deliverance and mine, for which, in any case, it cared not a jot.

On the seventh day (at seven in the evening), the angel Heurtebise became a poem and set me free. I was in a daze. I contemplated the shape it had taken. It remained distant, haughty, entirely indifferent to anything that was not itself. A monster of egoism. A solid mass of invisibility.

This invisibility built of fire-spitting angles, this icebound ship, this iceberg surrounded by water, will always remain invisible. Such was the angel Heurtebise's choice, its earthly form having a significance for it that it does not have for us. It is sometimes the subject of dissertations and other writings. It hides itself therein behind the exegesis. As they say, it has more than one trick up its sleeve. It had wanted to enter our kingdom. Let it stay there.

When I come to look at it, I bear no grudge, though I quickly avert my gaze. I am troubled by its great eye that stares without looking at me.

I find it remarkable that his alien poem (alien to all but my substance) can speak of me, and that the angel could make me speak of it as if we had known each other intimately for a long time. Which proves that, without my vehicle, this character was incapable of taking shape and that, like a genie of Eastern folklore, it could in the long run only inhabit the vessel of my body. For an abstraction, the only way to gain solidity while remaining invisible is to contract a partnership with us, to keep the greater share for itself, and to allow us but an infinitesimal portion of visibility. And, it goes without saying, the full share of recrimination.

Set free, emptied, and somewhat debilitated, I settled down in Villefranche. I had recently had a reconciliation with Stravinsky, in a sleeping car that we had shared. We aired our dirty linen, which had been quite dry and taut since *Le coq et l'arlequin*. He asked me to write the libretto for an oratorio, *Oedipus Rex*.[1]

He had become latinized to the extent of wishing the oratorio to be in Latin. The Reverend Father Danielou assisted me in this task, which reminded me of high school.

Stravinsky was living in Mont-Boron with his wife and sons. I remember a lovely little excursion in the mountains, which February had blanketed with pink trees. Stravinsky brought along his son Theodore. Our driver spoke in oracles, pointing his finger in the air. We nicknamed him Tiresias.

It was at this time that I wrote *Orphée,* which I read in the Mont-Boron villa in September 1925. Stravinsky was reorchestrating *Le sacre* and composing *Oedipus Rex,* whose music, he said, was to be as tightly curled as Zeus' beard.

I brought him the lines little by little, as I wrote them. I was young. There was sunshine, fishing, boating trips. After we had finished work I would walk briskly homeward, late at night, all the way to Villefranche. Heurtebise left me alone. It was now no more than a theatre angel.

Nevertheless, I notice in *Opium* strange coincidences that surrounded the Pitoëff production in June 1926, coincidences that followed one after another, and become quite serious in Mexico. Once more, from *Opium: "Orphée* was being performed in Spanish in Mexico. The Bacchantes scene was cut short by an earthquake, which destroyed the theater and injured several people. The hall was rebuilt and *Orphée* was again presented. Suddenly, a stage manager announced that the show would have to be interrupted. The actor playing Orpheus could not come out of the mirror. He had died in the wings."

Written in 1925, the play was to be performed in 1926, once I had returned from vacation. The second reading took place at Jean Hugo's, on the avenue de Lamballe. I can still hear Paul Morand saying to me, as he slipped on his overcoat in the hallway after the reading: "You've opened a funny sort of door. But your door isn't funny, not funny at all."

The next day, I had lunch with Picasso on rue La Boétie. Finding myself once again in the elevator, I looked to the brass plate. It bore the trademark Otis-Pifre. Heurtebise had vanished.

P.S. On the subject of hauntings and mischievous pranks—broken crockery and hails of pebbles—which in certain houses seem to be the work of a mysterious and very silly force, one should consult Emil Tizané's astonishing book, *Sur la piste de l'homme inconnu.*† It is the first documented study of these trivial but still unexplained phenomena that occupy the fringe of the phenomena we are discussing.

What is it that Picasso does, if not to transport objects from one meaning to another and to smash crockery? But his haunted house eludes police inquiry. It is only subject to art critics.

Furthermore, these phenomena were stripped of much of their mystery at the 1952 Exhibition of Domestic Sciences. A pastry dish rises from the table, floats about, then alights before the guests. It would be fair to say that the crowd is less entranced by the flying saucer than by the pastries it delivers. Only one child looks on fearfully, not daring to touch the dish for which he might well have been the guiding force.

Such phenomena are often at the root of the charges brought against poets. At the trial of Joan of Arc, the general staff was represented by a bishop who, rejecting any notion of the miraculous, attributed the phenomena to possession and unknown forces. Joan was as much a victim of these as of any travesty of foreign justice.

The minor phenomena described by Tizané give rise to countless inquiries, unjust punishments, provincial murders. The guilty party, speaking undetected through the mob, is never discovered. People suspect each other and, reluctant to accuse some *thing,* comfort themselves by accusing someone.

†Paris: Amiot-Dumont, 1951.

ON
CRIMINAL INNOCENCE

I would have preferred to hear you plead guilty. One can get a handle on the guilty; the innocent eludes us. He only gives rise to anarchy.

1ST DRAFT OF THE SCENE BETWEEN THE CARDINAL AND HANS, ACT II, BACCHUS[1]

PRESIDING JUDGE: *You are accused of being not guilty. Do you plead guilty?*

ACCUSED: *I plead guilty.*

PRESIDING JUDGE: *Have you committed a specific crime, falling within the provisions of the law?*

ACCUSED: *I have never done any good.*

PRESIDING JUDGE: *That won't help you. The good cannot be judged, it is not the concern of justice. In the eyes of the law only evil carries weight, and even then, I repeat, only if it is expressed in specific form. Now, you yourself have admitted to committing evil in an imprecise manner, which will not absolve you. It's nothing to be proud of! We have witnesses and proof. Have you ever killed, stolen, betrayed?*

ACCUSED: *No, but . . .*

PRESIDING JUDGE: *There we are, then.*

GAZETTE DES TRIBUNAUX

In Aix, during the exodus of 1940, I was acquainted with a young couple who were very close to the family that was sheltering me. Doctor M., with whom I was staying, lived in town.

Doctor F. and his young wife lived off the road in a little house, behind which an expanse of fruit trees and kitchen gardens stretched off into the countryside. This little house had belonged to the young woman's parents. They themselves had it from their own parents, who had had it from theirs. It went so far back that this house seemed to represent, in an era of insecurity, the very picture of continuity that is so rarely found.

We often called on and dined with one another.

The young wife fascinated me. Her beauty and vivacity could wilt at the drop of a hat. She would recover just as quickly. One would have said she was watching the swell of an ominous wave in the distance, filling her with dread, and that she was struggling to ignore its approach. She would take on a hunted look, her glance and her movements suggestive of someone who was prey to a specific threat. She would no longer listen or respond. She seemed to age so perceptibly that her husband would stare at her, and we would grow as quiet as he. The tension became unbearable. We would have to wait until the waves crested, smothered their victim, broke, and dissipated.

A reverse process would end the crisis. The young woman became charming once again. Her husband smiled and talked. Tension gave way to geniality, as if nothing unusual had happened.

One day I was talking with Dr. M. about our young friend, and I asked him if she were highly strung, or if he knew of any trauma in her past that might account for her symptoms. If, for instance, she had been the victim of violence, if some ancient fear were at the root of her present state.

The doctor answered that he believed it to be so, but that the only story he was aware of seemed very long ago and not at all conclusive. "Now," he added, "anything is possible. We know very little about what goes on in the labyrinths of the human body. What's needed is a psychoanalyst. It seems, however, that for reasons you will understand, Mme. F. refuses to undergo analysis. You may include in her condition the fact that she has no children, that she has already miscarried twice, and that the mere idea of another pregnancy throws her into fits that do nothing to help her disorder."

Here is the story that the doctor told me.

Our young woman was an only child. Her father and mother indulged her every whim. She had just turned five when her mother became pregnant. The delivery drew near, and the little girl had to be told to expect a little brother or sister.

"You know how people have the sad habit of hoodwinking their children, of plying them with fairy tales about their birth. I find these fairy tales ridiculous. My children know they come from their mother's womb. They love her all the more for it, and we thus spare them those schoolyard explorations and sordid discoveries of the truth." In short, the little girl of our story was living in deception, and the drama that follows springs from that fact.

Father and Mother wondered how to go about preparing a child highly protective of her privileges for the sudden arrival of an intruder, for the necessity of sharing the universe that she ruled to the point of refusing the pets she was offered, fearing lest her parents grow fond of them and deprive her of a portion of their love.

They told her, with a thousand niceties, that heaven was sending them a little boy or a little girl, it was not yet clear which, but that it *was* clear when, that she should share their joy at the great news, and that the heavenly gift was to arrive any day now.

They had feared a tantrum. They were wrong. The little girl did not cry. Her stare grew icy. Instead of wailing, she dismayed them with the kind of silence displayed by an adult when informed by a lawyer of his financial ruin.

Nothing is more immovable than a child's solemnity when it has made up its mind. Well might the parents hug her, cajole her, wrap the news in pretty words—their levity seemed ridiculous when confronted by this wall.

Right up until the delivery, the little girl set this wall against all initiative. Finally, the delivery monopolized the parents' attention, leaving the little girl free to lock herself in her room and stew in her own juices.

The young wife brought a dead child into the world. Her husband comforted her by emphasizing their daughter's despair. She would surely recover her liveliness when informed that, in the final analysis, they had turned down the gift because it had caused her pain. The ploy was unsuccessful. Not only did the little one fail to change her attitude, she fell ill to boot. A fever and delirium gave every indication of pneumonia. Doctor M. asked if some indiscretion had been allowed. Doctor F. could think of none. He informed his colleague of the young soul's recent distress. Doctor M. conceded that such distress might unleash a nervous breakdown, but it could not explain the pneumonia, for which the patient would have to be properly treated. She was treated and saved. Once she was out of danger, things took an unaccountable turn. No amount of affection was able to melt the ice. The convalescent was wasting away. Some mysterious evil had taken the place of the known one, and was continuing its work.

It was then that Doctor M., at his wits' end, suggested psychoanalysis. "A psychoanalyst," he said, "would dare to cross the threshold of a realm where science stops and acknowledges its incompetence. Professor H. is my nephew. He must become yours as well—at least, the girl must believe him to be so—and he must come to stay with you. I know him well enough to be sure that he'll collude in this little conspiracy."

The psychoanalyst had been preparing for his vacation. He allowed himself to be convinced to spend it in Aix, with his uncle. Every day, he would visit the young couple, questioning and befriending them. The little girl was suspicious at first. Little by little, she grew used to him and was even a little flattered by the attentions of this grownup who did not play the fool and treated her as an equal. She began calling H. her uncle.

Within four weeks of this treatment, she found her tongue again, and the mock uncle was able to chat with her.

One day, as they strolled together far from the family and servants at the bottom of the garden, without any warning, with the serenity of a defendant pleading guilty before the examining magistrate, the little girl divulged the secret that had been stifling her and seeking a way out of the dark.

Let us supplement what took place with what she said.

It was the night of the delivery. It had snowed the day before. The little girl could not sleep. She waited. She knew that by the morning, maybe by dawn, the gift would have arrived at its destination. She also knew that this sort of gift would require an elaborate, mystery-enshrouded family ritual. There wasn't a minute to lose.

Knowing just what she was about, she got up without turning on the light, left her room on the second floor, held up the hem of her nightgown, and crept down the wooden staircase. When a step creaked, she stopped, hearing the pounding of her heart. A door opened. She flattened herself against the banister made of braided rope. She could feel the wool scratching her neck.

An unknown woman, wearing a dress and a white cap, crossed the patch of light cast by the open door onto the hallway tiles. The unknown woman went into the dressing room adjoining the master bedroom, and shut the door. The other door was left open. It was the door of an incommodious little bathroom, where the mother used to do her hair, powder herself, pin up her cap and veils.

The little girl continued her descent, crossed the hallway, and slipped into the room which the unknown woman had just left, scared to death she would return on the instant.

On the dressing room table was a pin cushion bristling with hat pins, which were worn very long in those days. She pulled out one with a head of baroque pearl, and stole across to the glass-and-wrought-iron door. The heavy door was locked. It would have to be reached. She summoned up the courage to find a chair, climb up onto it, turn the lock, get down, and return the chair to its place.

Once outside on the stoop, she silently shut the door and peeked through the wrought-iron window, whose foot reached just to the level of her eyes. It was time. The lady in white was crossing the hallway. A gentleman in a frock coat was with her, waving his arms about. They disappeared into the bathroom.

The little girl did not feel the cold. She circled the house. In nightgown and bare feet, she ran through the flower beds, across the hard earth. The moon had sedated the garden. It was asleep on its feet, literally. Its familiarity, its honest little garden's simplicity, had become a sort of menacing entrancement. The stillness of an armed guard, of a man hidden behind the trees.

The garden made one feel as if it were on the verge of some evil deed.

Of course, the little girl was not aware of this metamorphosis, except in that she no longer recognized her garden crowded with hanging laundry, scarecrows, and graves.

She ran. She lifted her gown and clasped the pin. She thought she would never reach her goal. Her goal was the bottom of the garden, the very place where, in her own words, she is unfolding to the professor the story whose details we were subsequently to learn.

And it was undoubtedly the scene of the crime, as it were, that instigated her confession.

She stopped, recognizing the kitchen garden. Her blood ran hot and cold. The moon had not transformed the cabbages into some other, terrible thing. For the little girl, the terrible thing was that they were cabbages. They stood out, marvelously sculpted and magnified in the moonlight. She bent over and, without hesitation, sticking out her tongue in the manner of an attentive schoolgirl, stuck the pin into the first cabbage. The cabbage offered a grating resistance. So she pulled out the pin, firmly grasped the baroque pearl, and stabbed. One cabbage after another, she desperately stabbed. The pin began to contort. She calmed herself down and slowly, meticulously, she perfected her technique.

She would rest the point of the needle at the center of the leaves, where the heart curls back. With all her weight she would press down, driving her weapon in to the hilt. Sometimes the weapon would refuse to come out of the wound, and she would have to pull on it with both hands, often losing her footing.

Nothing discouraged her. Her only fear was that she might miss a cabbage.

Her need fulfilled, like Ali Baba's servant girl interrogating the oil jars, the murderess inspected her victims, assuring herself that none had escaped the massacre.

On her homeward journey she did not run. She was no longer afraid of the garden. It had become her accomplice. Without realizing it, the criminal aspect of the place reassured her, elevated her to glory. She was walking on air.

She was not even aware of the risks which the journey entailed. She climbed the stoop, pushed open the door, closed it, placed and replaced the chair, crossed the hallway after having stuck the pin back into the pincushion, climbed the stairs, went into her room and into bed. And her serenity was so pure that she straightways fell asleep.

The professor contemplated the cabbage patch. He was imagining the astonishing scene. *I stuck all of them, all of them!* the little girl had said. *I stuck them all, then I went home.* The professor was trying to picture the crime as it has just been related. *I went home. I was very happy. I had a good sleep.*

She had a good sleep and had awoken with a temperature of 104 degrees.

"Afterwards," the professor had explained to the young couple, "you told her that it's better to have only one daughter. She didn't believe you. She felt guilty. She had killed. She was sure of it.

"She's being eaten away by remorse. Since I have not taken the liberty, you will have to prove to her that children do not come from cabbages. I hope you have come to understand the result of such foolishness."

Doctor M. added that the parents only reluctantly concurred. They believed the truth was a sacrilege, and would stain their concept of an innocent childhood. Now they live in Marseilles. When they visit Aix, they can't help wondering where their daughter's nervous disorder and fear of miscarriage come from.

Do you think, I asked Doctor M., that this old story could be the cause? I can't say for sure, he answered, but I remember, once, when the girl was fifteen, her parents went on a business trip and left her in my care. My nephew came to visit for a week. By that time, the adolescent had learned not only that people are not born in cabbages, but also that my nephew was not a member of her family, but of ours. All of that, however, was ancient history. One evening, we misguidedly began stirring up old memories. "Do you know the truth behind the cabbage story?" my nephew asked me. "Well, the truth is, the little girl really did kill. Instinctively, the little girl used every voodoo technique there is, and voodoo is no joke."

We went on to discuss voodoo, and came to admit that certain evidence for it does exist.

"It's not impossible," I concluded. "Perhaps she did kill. The main thing is that she should never suspect it."

"The trouble is," the doctor went on, "my wife and

I discovered that the girl had been listening at the door."

P.S. A Freudian household. Madame X. enters the room where her nine-year-old daughter is drawing with a red pencil. The nanny is off in the pantry. Madame X. leans over. What is her daughter drawing? An enormous phallus.

Madame X. grabs the drawing and flees. She gives no heed to her daughter's howling. Monsieur X. comes home from his golf game. "Look at this." Monsieur X. throws a fit. "Where could the poor dear have seen such a thing?"—"That's what I'd like to know." I'll spare you the details of the investigation. After four days of upheaval, Monsieur questions his little girl. Her answer: "They're nanny's scissors."

ON
THE DEATH PENALTY

I have a greater sense of decency in emotion than in action, and if I am but rarely disgusted by unconventional behavior, I am conversely always discomfited when people start airing their dirty linen. I am never embarrassed by the sight of outward exhibitionism, while I find inward exhibitionism quite shocking. Furthermore, I find it highly suspect.

Which is why this diary is not a real diary.

I would find it almost fair that the law should safeguard outrages against the visible, while prosecuting outrages against revealed invisibility. But such provisions are not found in our statutes. (Of course, I am not referring to the trials of Baudelaire, Flaubert, etc., which had nothing to do with scandal. To my mind, the scandal was mendacity preferred as confession.) No less are poets guided by wise caution to hide their souls' shamelessness beneath a stylized disguise, and what offends me in a diary is not a whole procession of thefts and murders, but rather the motives for these murders, these thefts, and the searches they entail. It seems as if the guilty party is no longer tracked through town and country, but through a kind of gloom in which hunter and hunted are not easily distinguished the one from the other.

Some lie, delighting in exhibitionism (as is proven by the guiltless who offer false confessions), others confess indirectly by transferring their hidden instincts onto those they are interrogating. It is surely the pleasure taken in self-accusation without risk, self-immolation without pain, holding forth without fear, that drives the press and the public to gorge themselves on atrocity.

When a good crime bursts onto the scene, the papers' circulation triples. A mystery is always spun out when hypocrisy can feast itself on humanness. Public and principal players become equals in the drama. One thinks of a duel in which everyone is killed on the spot.*

During the trial of Leopold and Loeb, who were the precursors of the intellectual crime of which Hitchcock's film *Rope* represents a type of apotheosis, the defending attorney having said: "Every man carries within him the obscure desire to kill," and the judges having asked how they, the judges who punish murder, could be suspected of harboring such a desire, the attorney saved his guilty clients from the electric chair by crying out: "Haven't you been trying to kill Leopold and Loeb for the last several weeks?"

*After the events at Lurs, the police had to run off a family that was picnicking at the scene of the crime.

Man is merely following the rhythm of plants and animals devouring one another, but he devours himself under the aegis of legislation that tends to lead to legalized murder, the which, laying no claim either to impulsiveness or psychosis, is reminiscent of brothels where sex is transacted coldly and without passion.

The death penalty is unacceptable. Massacre is the only true law. The addition of specific laws to this chaotic one is a factitious procedure, a self-condemnation in others. Judges and juries should analyze themselves with the same solemnity they apply to running down and bringing their stag to bay. They should unleash a riot within themselves. They would probably be unhappy with the verdict, unless they should come to pride themselves on being their own hunting grounds, and on being able to break off the hunt before the hounds sink their teeth in.

At the Nuremberg trials, those who had established themselves as judges were the ones to be judged. High starched collars no longer offer the neck any protection against the rope. But we would have preferred a more immediate revenge. Such immediate justice spares a tribunal the task of punishing that which it respects above all else: discipline and obedience to one's leader.

In my case, it would be sheer boastfulness to exempt myself on the grounds that I would not kill a fly. I eat the cattle whose slaughterhouse torture I cannot suffer. And have I not, at times, secretly cherished the dream of some form of justice (my own) that would pound my enemies into dust?

It's easy enough to point a finger at those who bend under tyranny. And you can count on your fingers the number of citizens who disobey ruinous orders, knowing that disobedience would entail their own death. Such magnificent rebellions are few and far between. We should not forget to honor the patriots who proved exceptions to that rule in the Gestapo's chambers. Among others, our own Jean Desbordes, who had to avert his eyes from the scene of an accident, but died rather than talk under torture.

The glamor of flowing blood is a strange one. It's as if some sort of lava from our inner furnace seeks to identify with it. The sight of blood disgusts me. That hasn't stopped me from naming my film *Le sang d'un poète*,[1] from displaying blood therein at several instances, or from having recourse on numerous occasions to the Oedipal theme, which is drenched in blood.

It's as if we were revenging ourselves against invisibility's defenses by seeking to uncover the bubbling red sources within its domain. It's as if we had raised to cerebral level that bloody fascination of savage tribes, a fascination so strong that, on some islands, the natives cut each other's throats during the day, feast together at night, only to resume their carnage the next day.

But the mystery of our behavior becomes rather

distressing when validated by the gladiator's trademark. When it is surrounded by ceremony, when it becomes a gratuitous show to satisfy the primitive instincts of a complacent crowd.

One of the most awful incarnations of hypocrisy—other than its willingness to attack the vices it practices behind closed doors—is in the extremes to which the hypocrite is driven by his shame of lying, compelling him to pass his blushing off as indignation.

I must kill my brother. These are the thoughts of a culprit at liberty when face to face with a culprit seized. Perhaps this reflex satisfies the coward's need to punish himself in a surrogate.

People may retort that fiends must be suppressed. Despite everything, I am astonished that people lay claim to some higher justice, when every minute this higher justice proves itself to operate according to impenetrable statutes that undermine our own, eliminating the good, accommodating the evil, all in the name of some hidden arrangement in which man is not required to participate.

Nature pushes us to destroy *en masse.* Our destructive giddiness abets its imbalances, its inequalities, the tide of forces that drives its machinery. But I have a hard time believing that a criminal or a court of law can supplement it in any useful way. It functions in great waves, great events, in disasters that correct its faulty arithmetic.

To me, to be selected at random for jury duty seems the epitome of bad luck. What can be accomplished, sitting around like a host with a table-ful of unwanted guests? And isn't there sure to be one of those roughnecks to confront our doubts, boasting of his skill at carving the turkey? At this table, the turkey is a defendant whose neck is on the block. His own neck safe, our blustering roughneck gourmet would lure his guests to a cannibal feast.

What *humble* arrogance shines forth from a jury returning from its deliberations! And what distress from that unhappy man whose lonesome voice has found not one believer!

The discomfort we feel before such spectacles has deep roots, worthy of study. The Moscow Decree foresaw neither radio nor the filmmaker. The Napoleonic Code was unable to foresee psychiatrists. You will tell me that they are brought in for consultation. The verdict is thereby no less dependent on the mood and circumstances which sway the guests to the right or to the left, on a full stomach or an empty, unhearing stomach. Around our table, it is heart which the belly sorely lacks.

Reading G. M. Gilbert's book on the hidden side of the Nuremberg trials *(Nuremberg Diary),* one is stunned by the childishness of a coterie that sent the world into upheaval. We had placed it on a scale commensurate with our suffering. We had imagined its members bound by the sobriety of criminologists, by deep political convictions. Considerations of rank no longer constrain their relationships. They rejoice over passing the numbers test and ink-blot tests they are made to take. They have been deflated. They show their colors. What is it I see? Petty jealousies, inane grudges. A schoolyard overrun by louts and prigs. The abominable pranks of the schoolboys who thought up Auschwitz, Colonel Hess, the death of two and a half million Jews led through phony train stations to phony showers, with a quick stop before the oven doors. And the *it wasn't me, sir*s that every man heaps on his fellow's back. All this confirms my theory on the terrifying irresponsibility of those responsible, of that flaunting of responsibility illustrated by Chateaubriand's remark (which I quote from memory): "Bonaparte was in a runaway carriage that he believed himself to be driving."

Bergson would say that their fall has made stooges out of these captains, ministers, and diplomats. His successors would say that their fall has destooged them, and shown them as they really are. But the absurdity of their fall does not provoke laughter.

Eddington writes that events do not happen to us. We encounter them on our way.

We should understand that these predetermined events do not participate in our three dimensions. Their aspects are many. Their heteromorphic unity can be approached from a variety of angles. Free will and fatalism become entangled. For people tend to bow to fate, with the excuse that it has but one face. In fact, it has several mutually contradictory and interacting faces, like Janus' double profile.

It is most likely the belief that fate has but one face—similar to our own—that comforts juries after a sentencing to death. "So it was written." Perhaps, if indeed it was written, they should have read the writing in a mirror, and surprised themselves with what it said. They would have had the rare fortune of observing themselves, man and reflection, from both sides of the bar simultaneously.

What does a painter do to highlight the mistakes in the portrait he is painting? He inverts them in a mirror. The juror, returning home at night, confronts himself in the mirror. The mirror inverts him. It highlights the mistakes in his head. And his head pleads: "Were we not required to be critical? To prove our perspicacity? Not to show ourselves credulous? Not to let ourselves be convinced by the defense's rhetoric? By all-too-easy proofs? Were we not required to amaze justice with our righteousness? Should we have submitted to the whims of a room seduced by theatricality?

If I am censured (or congratulated) for having signed so many petitions for reprieve, especially those of my adversaries, I answer that I did not sign them out of the goodness of my soul, but because I refuse to see, in my inverting, reflecting mirror, a head crowned with the crime of responsibility.

In the final analysis, what is the role of an inflexible jury? To make the drama a flop. But we are not in a theater. The red curtain is the blade of a guillotine.

When laws cease to function and when, for instance, the people take the law into their own hands, or some blunder (as happened at the Champ-de-Mars)† permits any license, the primitive laws of blood take over. Impossible to save he whom the crowd has seized and is tearing to pieces. It's either the lance or the torch for him. The revolutionary ideologue exhausts himself in vain, exhorting the crowd to wait for justice. There's a different, cockeyed justice at work. And there is nothing to prove that, were the victim to elude his illegitimate executioners, this ideologue's justice wouldn't lead him to the legal executioner by a slower and even more painful path.

An ideology has its roots in popular instinct, to which it owes its success. But it wears the mask of legality, and even when it seeks to forgive, the fear of losing its platform and alienating the crowd suffices to put it back on track.

Only time can stanch its fevers. We then experience a relaxation, a fatigue, during which the machinery reverses itself. A nap saves the accused from life behind bars. In fact, they are benefiting from the ogre's digestive processes. The slightest victim would make it vomit.

It is certain that justice is incapable of objectivity. A court of law is a group of individuals inclined to subjective reaction. And if it is sad to see a studious pupil held back over one vote, it is positively dismal

---

†July 17, 1791. The National Guard, led by Lafayette, fires on a peaceful crowd to persuade them to disperse. Panic ensues, and many are trampled to death. Known as the "Massacre of the Champ-de-Mars."

that one unfavorable vote can send a man whose guilt may be in doubt to the chopping block.

One night, at the screening of one of Cayatte's films on this subject, I observed people's faces during and after the show. During the show, they seemed to be won over by its message. Afterwards, awakened from its collective hypnosis, the audience reverted to its mien of cannibals around the table. Each individual resumed the arrogance of nobility conferred by responsibility. It is likely that any member of this audience, proud of receiving an official summons, would forget the film and claim to himself: "Our duty above all." From that moment on, the defendant's life is hanging by a thread.

Nevertheless, I have noticed that, if the idea of a war submitted to the secret plans of nature receives a wide body of support, that of the death penalty is finding more and more objectors. Pamphlets and petitions are being circulated. And, just as today's youth is rising up and seems to want to break the sound-barrier—that is, the silence-barrier—so, too, myriad individuals are working together to spread the word of anti-racism and to oppose the death penalty.

To what extent these movements abet or hinder nature's cold machinations, I do not know. It is a mess that man observes without, alas, being able to clean up. One man's order is different from another's, and nature allows us freedom only to the point where our efforts do not clear up the carefully maintained disorder which is her order.

ON
A PURPLE PASSAGE

The schism between religion and science was a great mistake. A sort of ricochet of original sin. We carry the entire burden of this nineteenth-century mistake. We are responsible for it. Science, unable to see that the symbols of religion conceal numbers, is responsible. Religion, having forgotten numbers and stuck to its symbols, is responsible.

All that scientific arrogance, only to come back to Heraclitus, the triad, to the Trinity, of which the Father, the Son, and the Holy Ghost—symbolized by a patriarch, a young man, and a bird—are but conventional signifiers in the vocabulary of simpletons.

Many contemporary scientists are believers, and religion is gaining on science. It is a great pity that it is gaining, instead of holding science back.

The more science strives against the number 3, and against the number 7 (which combines the triad with the four paws set to earth by the nineteenth century), the more it respects the 0, and is astonished by the number 1.†

For if man dismembers the number 3 in destroying matter, it is only in small quantities, with the sole aim of destroying others' number 4 to the advantage of his own. To the 0 he restores this number 4 belonging to others, without understanding that the number 3, of which everything is made, is regrouping under his very nose and at his expense, and that the number 4's, whose powers are yet untried, will rise one day to threaten him.

The great flaming columns that rose above Hiroshima and Nagasaki were nothing but the wrath of the number 3, reintegrating itself and returning to a region in which man cannot meddle in what does not concern him.

Listen to what one of the pilots of the superfortress *The Great Artist* had to say, after having dropped the bomb: "I'm not so sure that we aren't playing around with forces that we have no business playing around with." Games that will be deadly up until the moment when, through excess of human stupidity that man insists on taking for genius, the number 1 will slyly urge him to play too hard with the triad and to return our poor world to the zero whence it came.

---

†Cocteau appears to be presenting his version of thirteenth century cabalistic writings. His idiosyncratic interpretation would seem to yield the following definitions: 0 = the Great Negative; 3 = the Universal Construct; 4 = Rational Materialism; 7 = Earth/Man/Spirit.

It took man centuries to regrasp the certain knowledge that space and time work in unison. Yet it seems an elementary observation that the amount of time it takes to approach a house diminishes in negative proportion to the increasing volume of the house, and that this house is only restored to habitable spatial dimensions when we no longer inhabit the period of time given us to reach it. There is an exchange of dwellings. One could not exist without the other, and even from a distance man must undergo strange contortions in order to recognize this tiny house and to imagine that he might fit within it.

I would reiterate that, to the human mind, when temporal perspective is dissociated from the spatial, it functions inversely to that of space, in which things grow smaller as they recede, while they grow larger as they recede in time. This is what distorts both childhood and historical events. They assume vast proportions through this phenomenon of magnification.

Time and space form a compound so elastic, so unusual, that man is constantly confronted with little proofs that confuse him and impede his understanding of it. For instance, when one of our film actors on set opens the door of a house from the outside, to shut it again only several weeks later in the studio, the screen shows him opening and shutting that door in quick succession. Our work in film is to skew the time-lapse in which the actor has lived his own life, in order to show him living a different one. It is true that the units of time and space that are cut up and repasted by the filmmaker remain whole. But is the compound of time and space distilled by this method so very factitious? I wonder. Reality sometimes makes use of it. For many a false testimony stems from an analogous agency, in which a man may be deceived by the distorting perspectives of time and space, and in perfectly good faith sends one of his peers to his death.

A certain kind of documentary film rubs our noses in our own shit, when it presents the plant kingdom by means of stop-action photography that results in an accelerated sequence of images.

When these images are projected at the correct speed, they reveal proof that the plant kingdom leads a highly turbulent, artful, erotic, and cruel existence. A disparity between its rhythm and our own had concealed this life from us, had beguiled us concerning the plant kingdom and its feigned serenity. Which leads us to conclude that all that we hold solid, stable, and inert swarms and ferments; that some inconceivably fast camera could reveal matter as it is, and show us nothing but wild rutting, hidden vices, opposites devouring each other, a vortex of attraction.

The first time that Germany sent us films depicting the plant kingdom at altered speeds, the French censors took fright, judging—with some justification—that they bore a close resemblance to the brothels of Marseille. The films were banned. They were given underground screenings. The resemblance left no room for doubt: the screen was invaded by images of sucking, male members, vulvas, sperm, and orgasms.

The string bean offered a less obscene medium. It writhed along the length of its pole. One might have thought it was licking itself, the way a cat licks its paws. It looked like a young monkey, a spritely and harmless elf.

As I was admiring its restlessness and gentleness, an old lady cried out from the shadows: "God! I'll never eat string beans again." The old dear! She'll be laid to earth, and soon be pushing up string beans of her own.

All of this would be funny if it weren't sad. One gets the distinct feeling that the more man learns, the more he seeks and believes himself to have attained the mystery, the further away he drifts, for he is slipping down a long slope of errors that he has no choice but to follow, though he supposes himself to be climbing up it.

Which is why religion has held science back and kept it secret, exploiting it only to strike at the crowd and hold it in awe. There's chaos as soon as the masses are involved. And here I was, blaming censorship; perhaps it was prudent not to complicate the teachings of Sigmund Freud by exposing the intimacies of flowers and vegetables.

It was a great wisdom that led the Israelites, when they were required to supply copies of their writings to the powers that be, to replace them with ciphers, and to disguise their social, economic, and scientific discoveries as fables. These fables became the credo of a Church that had come to question them by the sixteenth century, though without suspecting that they were the opposite of what should have been understood. The study of this lost cipher must have been brief, giving rise to misapprehensions already passed on by the translators of the translation (Luther's abounds with mistakes), requiring a deep knowledge of Hebrew, of its double and triple meanings. I would never have suspected any of this had not Mme. Bessonet-Fabre previously elucidated this cipher for me, and commented on the parables which thereby lost their dark sorcery and became surprisingly transparent.

These fables are tenacious. They were once the daily bread of a superficial Catholicism, the type that rises up against a pope who accepts them as fables and is more concerned with the ciphers they conceal.

Though the pope might give a speech in 1952 on the relationship between religion and science, the schism continues to exist, and that's a shame. Because it prevents priests from recapturing their primal privileges, and from preaching the gospel within a triangle inscribed with heart and eye.

We might then begin to perceive the implication of Christ's words: "In my Father's house are many mansions," and to understand that all religions are part of a whole, that while the order of the numbers might change, the sum remains the same.

And since the earthly machinery cannot but follow the universal, we would see a livable Europe— what am I saying?—a world in which man would respect the numbers that guide him, and would leave to nature the task of imbalancing herself (her levels). She would get by somehow, do her own laundry, with the help of epidemics, earthquakes, hurricanes, tidal waves, car accidents, aviation accidents, suicides, natural deaths and other sandbags she flings that are duly recorded by the press each morning. (In the *Journal* of 5 March, 1952: *The tragic accident of the Nice-Paris. Northern Japan ravaged by earthquake, followed by tidal wave. Railway disaster in Brazil. Smallpox in Marseille. Tornadoes rip through Arkansas, Alabama, Georgia. More dead on American roads than in Korea, etc.*)

But I digress. For it may be through his inability to admit others' beliefs and his obstinacy in imposing his own that man collaborates in nature's imbalances. Nature thus obtains from our wayward species the war-like rhythm which she effortlessly imposes on passive kingdoms. Man therefore imagines himself the victim of consecutive wars, without understanding that there is but one, with little rest periods that he mistakes for peace.

Let us return to our own case, the duel between the visible and the invisible, the reporting of which threatens to carry us away. And let that which follows be the logical prologue of a highly meaningful adventure in which the cipher-concealing fables served as an excuse to the forces that would like to see me invisible, and which concealed my cipher beneath images of scandalous visibility.

As I was finishing my play *Bacchus*, I felt that something was about to happen, though I couldn't guess what. I had even laughingly said to Mme. W., at whose home I was working: "Arm your ship, we'll soon be taking to the oars."

I should have been warned by an apparently humorous event that should compel us to acknowledge the medievalism of our era.

They had just burned Santa Claus at the stake in Dijon. The Church had accused him of being a dangerous, Germanic habit, likely to tempt children into sin. The poor children who believe in this fable will have to be burned alive as heretics.

In short, I could foresee a sort of "bother me and you're dead" imperialist attack on *Bacchus;* but I was unable to predict the angle of attack, from which window the shots would be fired, since my play offered a variety of targets to all and sundry. Furthermore, a play being highly visible, the invisible was compelled to deploy its defensive weaponry.

The sniper was François Mauriac, against all anticipation, since he was an old friend. Together we had built our first weapons, and I could not have conceived the possibility of his turning one of those weapons against me.

A certain kind of imperialism led the attack: that of Literature. It hid behind morality, of course.

The sniper's indiscretion was to have recently published an article (in *La Table Ronde*) in which he argued for the artist's freedom of expression and his right to say anything he chooses. His argument, however, was tailored to his own personal use.

We will see that the sniper was the type who takes aim very slowly, a type which I describe in *Le secret professionel*.[1] He misses his mark because he is chiefly concerned with striking a dramatic pose and with being noticed by the huntsmistress.*

As far as dogma was concerned, I was safe. I had consulted the Dominican and Benedictine authorities. They had given me their *exeat*. Santa Claus's pyre, and the first log set on mine by Mauriac, risk giving the Beast of the Apocalypse an unfortunate resemblance to God's Own Creature. The great luminaries of the Church disapprove of such goings-on. The bishops of Michel de Ghelderode and Sartre don't upset our secular judges. The arrow overshoots its target. As a precursor to mysticism (mysticism in the wild), sacrilege reassures them. Arthur Rimbaud will be allowed to profit by it.

I must be a better Christian than a Catholic. *Bacchus* is undoubtedly a Christian play. In his heart, Cardinal Zampi is less orthodox than Christian.
I admit to being shocked by the fig leaves on the

---

*This outward style, as if detached from the object, this painting that conceals the object and makes people say: "I don't always agree with Mauriac, but he does have a way with words!" Which cannot occur when style bespeaks an ethic, loses all decorative appurtenance and repels the insects that are strangers to this ethic. Human insects thus consider that "there's no style to it." They turn away from a true flower to pounce upon artificial flowers.

statues in the Vatican.** On the other hand, I would have found it quite normal that the treasure's gemworks should be hidden behind fig leaves. It made me think of a phrase of Maurras' cited by Gide: "I will not leave this wise procession of Fathers, of synods, of popes, of all the modern elite's great men, to attach myself to the gospels of four obscure Jews." Anti-Semitism could hardly be taken any further.

As usual, I am probably on the wrong side of the barricade. I think of Gide's credo: "I do not accept that anything could be harmful to me; on the contrary, I wish everything to be useful to me. I mean to turn everything to my profit."

This is the credo of visibility. In order to arrive at the credo of invisibility (my own), one has but to remove a negative from these sentences, and to adjoin these lines from Heraclitus: "For God, all is good and just. Men, on the other hand, perceive certain things as just and others as unjust."

What can I do? My factory is built that way. I hate only hatred, which I find nevertheless more justifiable than fickleness, of which I see a lot in my adversaries' attacks. I am almost sure that, were Mauriac to read my play and reread his open letter, he would be ashamed, and would run to cry on his confessor's shoulder.

**Doctor M. had just told me about a lady who had explained to her little daughter that she was forbidden to look at her little brother's "shameful parts," the root of all evil in the world. The little girl, having castrated her little brother with scissors one night, hastened to waken her mother and tell of her exploit. She thought herself a heroine, a Judith. She was astonished to see her mother crazy with grief.

I had wanted to write this *Bacchus* for a long time. I could see it as theater, film, book. I came back to the idea of a play, believing that the theater would best frame the story. I had gotten the idea from Ramuz.† In Vevey, the custom is still revived for the grape harvest.

This custom goes back to ancient Sumeria, about three thousand years before Christ.

> Documents describe the famous ceremonies performed at the dedication of the Temple of Ningirsou. The jubilant crowd abandons itself to veritable bacchanalia whose origins can be traced to the ancient agrarian cult. For seven days a general licentiousness rules the town. Civil law, like moral law, is suspended. No authority is wielded. A slave replaces the king, enjoys the liberty of the royal harem, is served at the prince's table by his servants. Once the feast is over, he is sacrificed to the gods, that they may absolve the town of its past sins and generate abundance. Before the temples, sacred mysteries are performed that will one day reach Babylon. Saturnalia and mysteries will survive throughout Mesopotamian history. Berosus bears witness to them in the third century. And Rome itself will celebrate these strange feasts, passed down from the depths of time, which Christianity will preserve in the Carnival.
>
> J. Perenne. *Civilisation antique*

My first version told of a dictatorship, in which a village idiot rose to become a monster. I soon gave that

†Charles-Ferdinand Ramuz, 1878–1947. Swiss novelist.

up. It was too rough, and in any case it resisted my efforts. I took on the subject of youth's confoundment by dogma, sectarianism, and other obstacles set before it. A prey to helping hands and feelings, youth tries to remain free. Its chaotic freedom dodges between the obstacles until they crush it. The only way it can overcome is through cunning or the assumption of power. Tact fails where deviation is required. Youth forges ahead. Its awkward straightforwardness, its daring, its heart, its senses, all play it false in a society ruled by deviation, where deviations silently slither and strike amongst one another.

Hans is sincerely and rashly committed, and deeply gullible. His act fools the bishop and the duke. It can't fool the cardinal, who is from Rome and has seen it all before. He pretends to be taken in so that he can learn more about the crises in Germany, where he is prospecting. He likes the duke and his daughter. He can sense the unrest that the Reformation brings to family life. "Say nothing that you can't take back." This is his advice to the duke. In the first draft, he added: "I wish that Christina would fall sick, since only unconsciousness can make your family keep quiet."

He is another of Stendhal's prelates. He is both refined and sensitive. He warns Hans: "You are like a moth to an open flame." He schemes to keep this moth from the fire. Unable to catch it in flight, he saves it from the flames, even after his own death. Through his final deed, the Church shows its clear-sightedness. Some Catholics have interpreted as mendacity the right that Zampi arrogates unto himself in order to remain worthy of his ministry and of his heart.

By the time Sartre and I learned that both of our plays were set in sixteenth-century Germany, it was already too late. He was finishing up *Le diable et le bon Dieu*[2] in Saint-Tropez, and I had just completed my first act in Cap Ferrat. I was on the road. We decided to meet in Antibes. Our plots had absolutely nothing in common. I could go on with my work. As our research covered the same territory, Sartre recommended some books which I added to those that taught me to know Luther. I was receiving such books from every direction.

The hard part was to take my notes, lock my files in a chest, forget about them, and to recapture their essence through the mouths of my characters.

These are old lines that sound subversive, being given a fresh angle. They're attributed to me. It is fair to say that they do coincide with what was going on in 1952, but I didn't become aware of the coincidences until much later. Some became appreciable to me only through the laughter or applause of the audience.

Claudel's *Jeanne au bucher* throws me off stride. The Church is one. Her greatness lies in pulling herself together. When she condemns Joan of Arc and then canonizes her, she seems to me just like a person who has made a mistake and repents. By canonizing Joan, she bravely points the finger at herself.

It is the nobility of this confession and recantation that I admire in her. If this were Captain Dreyfus instead of Joan of Arc, a review of the trial at Rennes would offer a playwright no chance to satirize the general staff. Unless the playwright were an antimilitarist or an atheist. Then he could attack both Church and general staff. But not if he respected them,* in which case he would praise their ability to reconsider an opinion. Any official body must be imagined as a body with a soul, fallible both as body and as soul, liable to falls from grace and to repentance.

Watching the play, I was surprised that Claudel's scenes could sneer at one Church and exalt another without shocking our judges, who were so harsh on my cardinal and his schemes. Though they would never accept the spoofing of a general.

The old fogey in *Les mariés de la tour Eiffel*[3] provoked an outrage and prevented the piece from being revived. He's just a vaudeville clown, neither more nor less.

One must therefore resign oneself to the fact that some works irritate, give off strange, distorting waves, incite injustice, and that there is nothing the authors of these works can do about it, except to understand that invisibility protects them, and requires a retreat the better to control its perspectives and its profile.**

*When the French *Salon des artistes* at first rejected Manet, Cezanne, and Renoir, only to accept them later, it was the same jury that had come to its senses.

**Why has *Tête d'or*[4] never been revived, if not that the work's invisibility is protecting itself?

At first, when the piece was done, I brought it to Jean Vilar. But as my schedule clashed with his, I brought it to Jean-Louis Barrault. In one month, I managed the direction, the set, and the costume design. The actors of the Théatre Marigny company, overwhelmed with work because of the switch, had reckoned my text easy to learn. They soon discovered that the tongue-twisting style I use to make the words flow requires an absolute respect for the least syllable. Otherwise, the fabric rends. They developed a taste for these grammatical gymnastics. Jean-Louis Barrault made a cardinal of great presence. One seemed to hear a prelate out of *La chartreuse de Parme*.[5] One seemed to see Raphael's young cardinal.

We performed first for a closed audience whose reaction was very favorable, second for a gala audience whose reaction was predictable, and third before the public and critics. It was a solid success. Its solidity was one in which people are deindividualized, leave their individuality in the cloakroom, and lose themselves in the collective hypnosis reviled by our critics. Our critics, conversely, are individualized, and close themselves off in a spirit of contrariness. It was to be expected. But invisibility needed even more than this to achieve its ends. The night of the gala performance, driven by some blinding, deafening force, François Mauriac thought he heard and saw a work that was not the one I had written; he was offended by it, and swept dramatically out of the theater as my actors and I were being called back. The next day was a Sunday, and the company was performing *L'echange*. I was resting in the country. I had guessed that

Mauriac would come out with an article, and passed my time working on a response.

The next day, his article appeared. An "open letter," a purple passage of yellow prose that evinces a complete misreading of the world I inhabit. The case against a fable that has nothing to do with me.

A man attacked at the Champs-Elyśees round-about must defend himself, even if it sickens him. I added a few finishing touches to my earlier response, and published it under the title "Je t'accuse" in the newspaper *France-Soir*. I could not reproach Mauriac his atavisms, his Bordelais origins. I reproached him the fault of prejudgment, of assuming the rights of a priest and sitting at God's right hand.

> It's a municipal law you cite, knowing not the universal. God is not your colleague, your fellow citizen, your companion; if he has communicated himself to you in any way, it is neither to lower himself to your level, nor to award you control of his power.
>
> Montaigne

The truth is, Mauriac has always been one of those children who like to mingle with the grown-ups. One sees this type at hotels. It's no use saying "It's late, go to your room. Go to bed"—they refuse to obey and bother everybody. (Mauriac himself has told me that he is "an old child, dressed up as an Academician.") Moreover, not being of the fraternity of minds that he would like to be, he is driven to writing articles about the members of that fraternity. The result is that, regardless of their contentiousness towards each other, they are united against Mauriac by his endless attempts to take part in their domestic quarrels and to set them against one another.

François Mauriac gets home from the theater. He sits down at his table. He is about to write his *Prière sur l'Acropole*. Strange prayer, stranger Acropolis. Strange reading for the Carmelites (Mauriac tells how they have been giving readings of his open letter). I would say, rather, that he has turned around, considered the man-hunting party at my heels, and put his horn to his lips in preparation of blowing a mort.

Nothing is worse than wounding your prey. It becomes dangerous. Mauriac has wounded his. But the prey is not dangerous, and he knows it. In the end, that is my only reproof.

My response was consciously anti-literary. I was not shooting to charm the huntsmistress. I had found the open letter's sweetness more cloying than its sourness. It reminds me of those ornamental cakes of my childhood, and of the figurines that ornamented them. I am shown tying my old mother to the post in Marigny (and insulting her). I am shown as an insect. I am shown as a satellite. I am shown in clown's costume, carried aloft by angels. Mauriac is no innocent, he knows very well that my work has nothing to do with Apollinaire's or Max Jacob's (except in the respect owed to them), and that my play is an objective study of the Reformation's premonitory symptoms; but it suits him to misalign the wheels so that the vehicle overturns. He's attempting an act of sabotage.

I suppose that Mauriac expected his hunting-horn solo, his harlequinade, to attract a following. He was wrong. Not only did the clergy not follow him (as I saw for myself in Germany), but he had pinned a scarlet letter on himself at the same time.

This scarlet letter's reputation has been spun out in congratulatory letters and articles that trouble me because I still believe that Mauriac bears little responsibility for what happened, that he was only the tool of those forces which I have been studying, of the shadow's wiles in its fight against the footlights and projectors.

It will be retorted that the play's success cripples my theory. I say that the interruption of the show following the company's departure on tour confirms it, that this is probably one of the reasons I chose the Marigny over other theaters that wanted *Bacchus,* and that would have performed it without alteration and without interruption.

I would add that I probably withdrew my piece from Vilar because the press was idolizing him to spite Jean-Louis Barrault, who had been the previous day's idol and was deidolized overnight, solely on the whim of this city that runs from idol to idol and has fun only when it's breaking its toys.

It was most likely this transfer of power and the

limited number of performances that caused me to make a choice against all logic and in secret obedience to orders more subtle than the visible world can issue.

A play is more convincing than a film because a film is a ghost story. There's no interaction between the audience and flesh-and-blood beings. The film's strength lies in advertising my thoughts, to substantiate them with a subjectivism grown objective, by actions that are irrefutable because they are taking place before your very eyes.

Thanks to this clumsy vehicle, one can manage to make the unreal seem realistic. This realism, however, overtakes the unreality, conceals its ciphers, and leaves the audience at the door.

One of my correspondents denounces my filmmaking, claiming that I allow too many people to see what should remain hidden. I explain to her that the film quickly muddles these secrets, delivering them only to the rarest of people, mingling with the crowd distracted by the rioting images. All religions—I will say it again, of which poetry is one—protect their secrets with fables, and reveal them only to those who could never know them were they not spread by fables.

In the theater, side by side, the audience unleashes a wave that washes over the stage, from which it washes back the richer, providing that the actors are actually moved by their simulated emotions and aren't just aping them, which would block the ebb-tide.

My *Bacchus* company, all worked up by foolish

criticism, gave it their all to convince. They were successful.

It remains no less true that it would be madness to be blinded by success. Misunderstandings arising from our success should be no more notable than those that bring us jeers. Otherwise we would fall back into the pride of responsibility. We would lose that haughty indifference of trees, an indifference from which I scold myself for descending all too often.

The soul is pathetically weak. Its main weakness lies in believing itself strong, to be convinced of it, when its very experience shows it to have no claim to the forces that emanate from within it, and that turn against it as soon as they see the light of day.

Note, 19th October, 1952—*Bacchus* at the Dusseldorf Schauspielhaus, with Gründgens spectacular as the cardinal. Surrounded by the endless ovations of this either extremely Catholic or extremely Protestant audience, and reading the notices the next day, I was honestly forced to ask myself whether the French and Belgian presses might have been the victims of a phenomenon of collective hallucination.

Second Note—In a hotel, a priest who takes a dying man's groans for erotic ones, and raps on the wall instead of coming to his aid—this is what Mauriac's articles against Genet make me think of.

What frivolity beneath these uniforms and these honors! Frivolity denouncing itself in others and relying only on the visible.

ON
PERMANENT LADIES

When I was overseeing the dyeing of the actors' hair for my film *Orphée,* I found myself eagerly eavesdropping and listening to those ladies who, deafened by their hairdryers, shout without realizing they can be heard.

We live in a world where questions of the visible and the invisible, of responsibility and irresponsibility, are not asked. A world faithful to the number 4. This world reminds me of the little girl's description of a cow: "A cow is a big animal with four legs that go all the way down to the ground."

Our ladies sit in their assuredness of being there. The Pharaonic helmet of the dryer lends them an air of royal power, of permanence through permanents. Of Delphic sibyls. They bake. They smoke. Oracles fly from their mouths.

A lady points out to her manicurist a young girl reflected in several mirrors. "The poor thing! Her mother gives her a million a month. How can you expect her to live on that?"

A helmeted Minerva confesses to another: "Me, I'm only sensitive to little things. I hold up bravely under the big things. You saw how I held up under the deaths of my sons. But I'd go mad if I ran out of butter. It's a funny thing. It's just my nature."

Pointing out a sick employee, one lady patient cried out: "Look at her complexion. She's a dead woman! Dead!" The sick employee overheard her and broke down.

I could give many examples of this naive egoism. I thought of the gala performances to which the permanent ladies are always invited. And I drifted back to my humble interpreters, who were going from brunette to blond at the technicians' insistence. I pictured the film, a veritable tunnel of mirrors I was about to enter, and that theater, forced upon us by our producers, whither these ladies and their husbands come to sit, proud of their ringlets.

During the German occupation, our ladies were permanently waved through the agency of some poor devils pedaling away in the basement. Their legs generated the electric current.

Here, the shadow dies a stranger to the body it perfects. One hand in a bowl of warm water, gaze locked on their own image, intent on the metamorphosis, on the work from which they expect a transfiguration, unable to dig within themselves, how could these ladies be expected to dig deeper still, to empathize with the invisible host tending to their needs? And yet, the fuel that drives their rudimentary machinery is the same as that which drives the complex machinery of genius. They have a soul. They have *soul*. And it is thanks to this soul that their vehicle works, in which the invisible resembles the visible. The patience of such vehicles is boundless when it comes to the hope of external progress. When it comes to internal progress, they are exempt on the strength of self-satisfaction.

For if some miracle were to occur, if in their own way the cyclists were able to generate some kind of moral light, some fear, some disquiet, some remorse, a breakdown of the machinery would reveal them to themselves as the helmeted voids they really are. The terror would cause their hair, as one of them put it, to "stand up and curl." They would die in their seats, their mouths open in the shape of a scream.

This is the audience to which we are condemned by an ancient indolence obstinately claiming it to be an elite. Money has changed hands and the elite has changed places. It has become legion. It throngs to the theater galleries where the couples, arm in arm, listen and watch instead of looking at each other. It transcends itself very well, sending out waves that enrich the performance. It collaborates. It does not revile what is offered. It reviles the theaters whose doors are shut to it by the price of their tickets.

We can never thank Jean Vilar enough for his enterprise. It is an enterprise to which I attach great historic importance. In his productions of *Le Cid*[1] and of *Le prince de Hombourg*[2] one finds what one had feared to be lost. I also found it in Germany, where the audience arrives, doesn't leave until the end, and gives its artists their due.

For the permanent ladies and their husbands arrive in the middle of the first act. They hurry off to the clubs before the end to meet their peers and to pass judgment on what they have just come from not seeing.

It seems likely that the cyclists' exhaustion from stationary pedaling gave rise to dreams that were a good deal closer to our own than to the nebulous daydreaming caused by dryer fatigue.

The young girls working in these hells where our ladies heroically bear their tortures, speak of how such torture leads to confidentiality. It awakens the psychoanalytic faculties. What is divulged by the invisible, however, is illustrative only of what is seen. The cauldron overflows. The young listener is of the same species as the hidden cyclists. She is anonymous. She is a mere garbage dump.

The permanent ladies drain themselves of their emptiness, and that completes the sitting. It is a double therapy from which they emerge all shining new. Taking off the white gown, they imagine themselves to have left within the young girl and within the dryer the color of their soul and of their hair.

Mlle. Chanel, who knows a thing or two on this subject, arrives on the coast after having attended Vilar's production of *Le prince de Hombourg*. She tells me how two of these baked ladies were beached behind her, highly fearful of the surrounding youths, whom they believed to be Communists.

One of the ladies referred to the program. "The playwright was a Kraut," she whispered to her neighbor. "His name was Kleist, and he killed himself." "So much the better," said the other one. "At least that's one less of 'em."

ON
A JUSTIFICATION FOR
INJUSTICE

"Another who stands accused, Cocteau . . ."
SARTRE. SAINT GENET

Youth is unjust. It owes it to itself to be so. It must defend itself against stronger, invading personalities. First it surrenders, then it goes on the defensive. From one day to the next, it has set up resistance. The love and trust within it now seem like a disease. In its haste to fight off this disease, it finds itself defenseless. It improvises. It turns against the object of its trust and tramples it, all the more violently that in trampling, it tramples itself. In this, it mimics the murderer who slashes away at a dead body.

It would be most unseemly of me to complain of youth's iconoclasm. When I was young, did I not impugn my loves? And above all, Stravinsky's *Sacre*, which infected me to the point where I took it for a disease and sought to provide against it. Youth forever aspires to replace one idol with another. One might well ask me (as did Stravinsky in the sleeping car in the "Birth of a Poem" chapter) why I have never attacked the idolization of Picasso. What Stravinsky meant to say was: "Since taking the offensive has been a defensive instinct in you since adolescence, why has Picasso, who has completely overrun your territory, never aroused that instinct?" The reason surely stems from Picasso's matador-like ability to switch directions so readily, his red cape to your right when you thought it to your left, his banderilla unexpectedly plunging into your neck. I loved his cruelty. I loved his disparagement of that which he loves. I loved his outbursts of tenderness that made you wonder what they were hiding. No one took better care of his bees, wore more masks, took more pains to uproot his swarm. All of this can distract the enemy that a youth in love carries within him.

Maurice Sachs had such persuasive charm that it continues to assert itself after his death. I couldn't say how or where we met. He rarely left my house. He hung around the clinics in which my health compelled me to live for long periods. His warm, wide-open face was so familiar to me that I can't pin a date on the memory of it. If he robbed me, it was in order to buy me gifts. And if I speak of robbery, it's because he did himself proud by it.

When Maurice was penniless, he would stuff his pockets with toilet paper. He would rustle it so that his pockets seemed filled with thousand-franc notes. "It gives me self-confidence," he would say.

I could not possibly whine about being duped. It's nobody's business but my own. I have always preferred thieves to the police. He is not robbed who freely gives. Even then, trust must be paramount, and so it was with Sachs. I repeat, he gave more than he took and took in order to give. Such a style of thievery can no more be equated with the sordid kind than with the kind that employs such imaginative genius that there is no analogous genius to protect us against it.

One year when I was staying in Villefranche, Maurice carried off the entire contents of my room in Paris in a cart. My books, my drawings, my correspondence, my manuscripts. He sold them shamelessly by the bundle. He could imitate my handwriting to a tee. I was still living on the rue d'Anjou at the time. He showed up at my mother's with a fake letter in which I gave him free rein.

While he was pushing one collection on Gallimard, the volumes of Apollinaire and Proust—the cover pages of which bore inscriptions to me by the authors—were doing the rounds at the auction houses. They were displayed in the windows. Since I was being held accountable for this outrage, I broke the truth to Gallimard. He called Sachs to his office and told him he had no choice but to fire him. Sachs asked for a few minutes. He vanished, reappearing with a letter from me, the ink still fresh. This letter begged him to sell off my books, correspondence, and manuscripts as soon as possible. "You see," Maurice

declared, "how I forgive Jean his delusions. I am burning his letter." He took out his lighter and burned it. In
relating this conjuring trick to me, Gaston Gallimard
told me that it was the burning of the letter that finally
convinced him. We laughed at Maurice's skill in exon-
erating himself by destroying false evidence.

Even exposed, Maurice would continue to cajole
his victims. He started from the principle that people
enjoy others' misfortunes without ever worrying that
they might be next. During the occupation, Jews
would entrust him with their furs and jewelry. And if I
were asked how I felt when told by the bookshops here
on the coast that they were holding suspicious merchandise, I would say I had *la cagne*. *La cagne* is an
affliction commonly found in Toulon. In olden days,
the port admiral's carriage would pass around a *cag-
nard* asleep on the road. *La cagne* is phlegmatism, the
farniente of the Italians. Maurice, too, had *la cagne*.
His *cagne* was wily. It would fatten him up, and then
he'd allow his own weight to pull him under.

Just before he left for Germany, he called me
one morning after a year's silence. He lay dying in the
Hotel de Castille. He begged me to come to him.

I found him in bed, very pale, at the Hotel de
Castille. "I have never loved anyone but you," he said.
"Your friendship was suffocating me. I wanted to deny
it. I have written lies and insults about you. Forgive
me. I have ordered them to be destroyed."

Maurice did not die in the Hotel de Castille. He
met his death in Hamburg, under abominable circum-

stances. His books were not destroyed. On the contrary, some are being published by our mutual friend, Yvon Belaval. Others are pending. They are owned by Gerard Mille.

I do not share my friends' opinion that these insults-are upsetting. Maurice told me the truth, his own, as any truth is our own. I consider his insults to me as proof of a profound impression. In any case, that is how I see them. As I have unmasked him at the beginning of this chapter, he goes for any weapon he can find and assails me willy-nilly with it. One can tell that he believes nothing of what he affirms. And whoever does not understand why he abuses me and himself, cannot understand his writings. He is fueled by that relentless need to eject that which bloats him. His technique is defensive and offensive. His race towards death—easily mistaken for flight—is its consecration.†

Maurice Sachs is a typical example of self-defense against an invader. The more he offends the more he beats himself. And he beats his chest, too, according to the rites of his fellow worshippers before the Wailing Wall. It is because of this whirlwind of blows that he is fascinating, and to it that he owes his posthumous success. But his cynicism would be of no

†Sachs eventually met an awful death. A Nazi collaborator in Paris, he moved to Germany during the war and became a Gestapo informer. Arrested, he was sent to a prison camp, where he also worked as an informer. He was executed in a forced march to Kiel during the Allied advance.

interest to anyone if it were mere confession and lies. It is interesting because it is of a passionate nature. Maurice had a passion for others and for himself. His works are the battlefields of his struggle between these two feelings. His youth prevents him from sustaining the two together. If he wants to live, he must kill. But it's only the visible person that he goes for. The other eludes him.

Long was the road that led him to this technique. He gave himself over honestly and disinterestedly to friendship. Of his friendship, neither Max Jacob nor I had any cause for complaint. He respected us. He never addressed me with the familiar *tu,* as I did with him, and youth does not generally grasp such implication. I was often made uneasy by the way very young poets would use the *tu* with Max Jacob.

After *Le Potomak,*† I decided to build myself an ethic. But it was far from complete when I went on the offensive. Maurice's ethic did not exist. With great dexterity, he abruptly decided to fashion himself a negative one. An ethic lacking ethics. From that moment on, he applied all of his active laziness to it. None of us suspected that he was writing continuously. We never saw him writing. It is true that he had begun to write at a time when my friends' attitude had compelled me to renounce his company.

Maurice wrote relentlessly. He told his own story. He dared to define himself by flaunting his so-called

†Jean Cocteau, *Le Potomak* (novel); 1919.

"turpitude," which is in fact mere obedience to those instincts that reject popular morality. As for the confessions about his sexuality, nature grinds morals in her mill. The films on the plant kingdom, of which I spoke earlier, are informative in that regard. It is through a hazardous use of sex that nature fluctuates between thrift and prodigality. For if her creatures abused for its own sake the pleasure that accompanies the reproductive act, her domicile would soon overflow. She urges visual disorder, to protect her invisible order. Such a wise disorder was once noted in the Pacific Isles. Young natives did their duty with restraint, and women gave birth in cowpats so that only the strong babies would survive. Up until the Europeans came to bring order, that is to say clothing, liquor, sermons, overpopulation, and death.

Sachs doesn't need to go that far. He is on his own downward slope. This slope may one day provide an edifying story to the court whose sentence is feared by so many young people believing themselves guilty. I know that he boasts and deceives. But on the whole, reading between the lines, I must commend the way he shows up the hypocrites by determinedly giving false testimony so as to reveal the truth.

When I try to recall Maurice, it is not in his books that I find him. It is during those thrilling years when literary politics divided our numbers, throwing us together and pitting us against one another. Maurice skipped from one camp to the other. He did not betray. He listened, laughed, helped, split himself asunder in order to be useful. I scolded him quite often.

When he entered the seminary, I warned Maritain. I knew he was entering to escape his debts. But Maritain went a step further. His nobility put high hopes in this sanctuary. He would save Maurice from worse debts still, debts that would be forgiven him. Maurice became a seminarist. We saw him in his cassock, bringing American cigarettes and a bathtub into his cell. His lovely grandmother, Mme. Strauss, was deeply concerned about his being able to wash there.

One day in Juan-les-Pins, when he was behaving particularly badly, I suggested that he return to civvies. He was already bored in the role. He graciously conceded, and such was his charm that the Reverend Father Pressoir, the provincial of the seminary, reproved me for being "too readily in need."

Poor Maurice. If he had not been the avant-garde of an era that lionizes all sorts of commandos, what would be known of him? I praise him for having made his weaknesses seem like strengths. Willingly or not, my ethic compels me to condone his, and to welcome him into my Pantheon.

Claude Mauriac provides me with a second example.

His father had been my friend from youth. I therefore adopted him like a son. At that time I was living on the place de la Madeleine. My house was open to him. If one wishes to enter my house, one enters. If one likes it there, one stays. I refuse to make provisions. And when I am asked what I would take from my house if it were burning down, I answer: *the fire*.

At Versailles, where I was beginning *La machine à ecrire*,[1] and whither he had joined me, he asked if I would mind if he took notes on what I said. It upset him that I was so poorly understood, and he was planning a book about me. I was able to prevent the note-taking, which bothers me. I was not able to prevent the book, as it was offered in good faith.

This book is well known. Friendship shines through the insults and inaccuracies. Claude lies, and arms himself by accusing me of mendacity. He would tell one reporter that he loved me, and that his love was patently obvious. He would later give me the proof. We met again on Saint Mark's Square in Venice, after a private screening of *Les parents terribles*. I forgave him all the more easily in that I find quarrelling distasteful, and that I knew the motives for his behavior. With Sachs, I had simply dismantled the machinery.

Claude praised *Orphée* in two wonderful articles. But the instinct was still there. He could not bring himself to follow his heart. He published a new article in which he recanted, claiming that *Orphée* is cheapened by an unreceptive audience. The normal thing would have been to attack the audience. He attacked the film. It so happens that the patience of my ethic is boundless, and I hope that Claude's tergiversation leads him one day to forge his own. Sachs's would not suit him.

I daresay he regretted this last article. A recent letter from him leads me to believe so. The *Bacchus* affair prevented any resumption of this hot-and-cold therapy.

Maurice's and Claude's attitudes are not alike, yet they fit together. Maurice babbles. Claude broods. In them we see the signs of youth closed off to impulse. This fear of impulse is often found in young people as the "anxiety of the act" noted by psychoanalysts. An anti-impulse thrusts itself into the gap. It wastes its energy in the fear of letting go and of being discovered. Shame prowls, hurling abuse. Goodness becomes synonymous with foolishness, nastiness with intelligence. As Hans says to the Cardinal in *Bacchus:* "Therein lies the drama."

Age brings us a robust health that no longer fears invasion. Should we be invaded by foreign bodies, we have learned to retrench, and to excavate a void that they will infect without contaminating ours. We are no longer afraid to admire contradictory works. We no longer seek to triumph over them. They become our guests. We give them a royal reception.

Gide was obeying the machinery of youth. He was caught up in it to the end. I would not mention him in this chapter if he did not clarify its meaning by his use of techniques that are unconscious in youth, but perfectly conscious in him. His yearning for youth entangled him in intrigues that made him forget his age. He would then behave with a frivolity that he would later be compelled to justify. He therefore provides me with a marginal third example, all the more striking for its wily defenses and barbed weaponry.

In this chapter wherein I seek to exonerate my aggressors, I feel compelled to enlarge my frame of reference, to find excuses for Gide's attacks on me in his diary, to determine the contributions of the young vehicles who passed between us.

In 1916, I had just published *Le coq et l'arlequin*. Gide was offended by it. He was afraid that young people would turn away from his curriculum, and of losing subscribers. He called me up like a naughty pupil before the headmaster, and read me an open letter intended for me.

People write me a good number of open letters. In Gide's, I was depicted as a squirrel, and Gide as a bear at the foot of the tree. I jumped wildly from branch to branch. In brief, I was getting a dressing-down and had to receive it in public. I told him that I intended to answer this open letter. He sniffed, nodded his approval, and told me that nothing was richer or more edifying than these exchanges.

It was to be expected that Jacques Rivière would refuse to publish my answer in the "Nouvelle revue française," in which Gide had published his letter. It was fairly severe, I admit. In it, I mention that Gide's house, Villa Montmorency, does not face outwards, that all his windows look out onto the back.

Gide had already received a scolding like this before. It had come from Arthur Cravan, whom he had used as a model for Lafcadio.[2] Cravan was a languid colossus. He would come to see me, stretch himself, spread out, his feet above his head. He had entrusted me with some pages in which he describes a visit Gide made to his garret, a visit very similar to that of Julius de Baraglioul.†

But, as was his custom, Gide had managed to profit from these pages and that visit. There was no profit to be milked from my response, except to answer it, which he did not fail to do. He adored notes and memos, answer for answer. He answered mine in the "Ecrits Nouveaux" which had published it.

Dare I confess to having not read it? I was determined to remain alert against a certain reflex, against a terrifying avalanche of open letters. Time went by. Along came Montparnasse and Cubism. Gide remained aloof. He knew how to forget injury, especially when it flowed from his own pen. He called me, asking me to take—let's call him Olivier—in hand. His disciple Olivier was "bored by his books." I would introduce him to the cubists, to the new music, to the circus whose great orchestras, gymnasts, and clowns we so loved.

I complied, with some qualms. I knew Gide and his almost feminine jealousy. Now, young Olivier

†A central character in Gide's *Lafcadio's Adventures*.

greatly enjoyed upsetting Gide, singing my praises into his ear, telling him how he rarely left my side and how he knew *Le Potomak* by heart. I did not hear of this until 1942, before leaving for Egypt. Gide confessed, and admitted that he had wanted to kill me (*sic*). It was from this story that all the muckraking in his diary stems. At least, so he claims.

He did not admit that I had had the greatest difficulty in persuading him to read Proust. He thought of him as a society writer. Gide certainly begrudged my having convinced him, once Proust had filled the *Nouvelle revue française* with his delightful, spidery writing. It swarmed over rue Madame. It could be deciphered on several tables.

The day Proust died, Gide whispered to me at Gallimard's, "Henceforth, I will have only one bust here."

His personality was a mixture of Jean-Jacques Rousseau the botanist, and Mme. d'Epinay's Grimm. He reminded me of that endless, harrowing hunt at the heels of a clumsy prey. He combined the fear of one and the cunning of the other. Both pack and prey lived within him.

Jean-Jacques's posterior is the rising, Freudian moon. Gide is not revolted by such exhibitionism. But if you turn it around, you can detect Voltaire's smile.*

---

*In answering my question about why he refused to get to know Gide, Genet said: "One is either the accused or the judge. I don't like judges who lean amorously over the accused."

I will not linger over those responsible for the inaccuracies that distort my slightest gesture. I have explained myself elsewhere. In speaking of Gide, I was thinking only of the labyrinth into which he drew the young, and in which he enjoyed losing himself with them. The machinery of rebellion was started up after his death. Abuse was heaped upon his corpse. Which is his one saving grace. He had been too exploited, commented upon, excavated, drained. His invisibility had become nothing but studied visibility. He will benefit from the iconoclasts. He can shelter in their shade. He had confessed the little things so as to conceal the great. The great will rise up to save him.

I loved Gide and he annoyed me. I annoyed him and he loved me. We're even. I remember that when he was writing his *Oedipe*,[3] after I had written mine *(Oedipe roi, Antigone,[4] Oedipus Rex, La machine infernale)*, he let me know about it by saying: "There is a veritable 'Oedipemic.'" He excelled at enunciating the syllables of difficult words. He seemed to draw them from some sort of cistern.

Towards the end of his life, he came with Herbart to my country house. He wanted me to direct the film based on his *Isabelle*.[5] From Herbart's looks, I could tell that he was floundering. The film was mediocre. I explained that to him in a written memo, and that it was rather hoped that he would do a film on *Les faux-monnayeurs*[6] or on *Les caves*.[7] He exulted, hearing me read from the memo. He pocketed that memo. It might even still be lying in a drawer somewhere.

Our relations were cordial to the end, right up until Jean Paulhan's letter described him to me, petrified on his death bed.

It remains no less obvious that there are those capable of giving offense, and those who must swallow it. I will be taken to task for attacking my aggressors. I am not attacking them. I am looking into their responsibilities and irresponsibilities. The visible and the invisible prevail together. Gide, Claude Mauriac, and Maurice Sachs—they have delayed my dissection and the sucking of my marrow. They have helped me unwittingly.

Moreover, I believe that the emanations that provoke attacks of a particular kind come far more from the accused than from the judge. In a field where litigation of responsibility does not exist, judge and accused are as responsible and as irresponsible as one another.

ON
RELATIVE FREEDOMS

"I am happy to exhibit, but not to put myself on exhibition." This was my answer to the Parisian reporter who suggested I exhibit my paintings in Paris.

For once, I was able to serve invisibility while also serving myself. Something rare enough that I took advantage of it.

I had the chance to see my paintings and tapestries hung (rather than hanged) on the walls of the new Munich Art Gallery (Haus der Kunst). An alert crowd milled about, studying them. In Paris, I'm familiar with the old refrain: "What's he up to this time? Why is he painting? Who gave him the right to paint?" And other niceties which I'll refrain from repeating.

I am not a painter, nor do I boast of being one. I painted because I was taking a rest from drawing, because drawing is a form of writing and writing sometimes tires me. I painted because I was fashioning myself a new vehicle. I painted because I enjoy the act of painting. It eliminates intermediaries. I painted, believe it or not, because I wanted to paint.

I may well give it up, should this vehicle disturb my omnipotent night, which dislikes having to expose its face to the daylight, to show itself in broad daylight, its face painted.

These paintings and tapestries will live as they please, will suffer and go about like people, free to go whither they will. As I write these lines, they are travelling from Munich to Hamburg, from Hamburg to Berlin, where other galleries and other stares await them.

Two sweet summers (those of 1950 and 1951), two summers when I tattooed the Villa Santo Sospir like a skin, and when I later took up the painter's tools. Two summers when I became wall and canvas, when I followed my own orders, without any judgment being passed down upon me.

Between us, it's the least I deserve. Destroy my paintings and you destroy me. Our visible forms can be destroyed. Our perspective on time and space prevents the destruction of their invisibility. For a work overflows its own existence. It projects itself even when destroyed. The ruins of Knossos are scented by such works.* What remains of Heraclitus? And yet, he speaks to us, he is our friend.

---

*At Knossos, the domed hives of the Cretan hills give way little by little to the palace's own open hive, a veritable labyrinth, which Daedalus built for Minos. The frescoes show us wasp-waisted people going from flower to flower, making perhaps that golden honey of which the pendant in the Candia Museum—the one on which two bees face each other—is made.

When I write, I disturb. When I show a film, I disturb. When I paint, I disturb. When I exhibit my painting, I disturb, and I disturb if I don't. I have a knack for disturbing. I am resigned to it because I would like to be able to persuade. I will be disturbing after my death. My work will have to wait for that other death, the slow death of my knack for disturbing. Perhaps it will emerge victorious, unencumbered by me, liberated, youthful, sighing with relief. This has been the fate of many undertakings that I respect, a fate that seems unlikely in this age that believes itself omniscient, farsighted, possessed of an eagle eye. For invisibility has countless tricks at its disposal. It is a conjurer, and never performs the same stunt twice.

How to paint without being a painter? I mean to say, a born painter. One of those painters who elude analysis. Auguste Renoir is the standard, a gnarled tree that flowered in all weather. At the end of each day, he would wipe off his brushes on little canvases that became masterpieces, of which I own a few. Someone said to Renoir: "You must be proud that your works command such high prices in the auction rooms." And Renoir answered: "One does not ask a horse if it is proud to have won the steeplechase."

All one can do is to set oneself a tricky problem and try to solve it. To picture the idea for a potential painting, and to copy that idea until the painting resembles it. To arrange a meeting between the abstract and the concrete. Lacking knowledge (or foreknowl-edge), to draw out a light from within oneself and to diffuse it as best one can. Our shadow does not de-spise a new machine. It tyrannizes us less. What serenity! And from this serenity, something is born. Good or bad, the painting I had stared at stares back at me, and I no longer dare to look at this staring paint-ing. Moreover, it grows weary. It begins leading a disquieting life that breaks away from our own to mock us. Little matter what it symbolizes. It has si-phoned off our deepest forces, from which it drains a youth our old age pesters to death. Even this youth it disdains, dreaming of striking out on its own. It strikes. And here am I boasting of being free to exhibit or not to exhibit my paintings. They are free to disobey me.

What a strange book this is! It flouts me. It repeats itself. It pushes me every which way. So as to bite its own tail, it makes a circle of the same words written over and over. How onerous are the words *visibility* and *invisibility* to me! How I wish I could unburden the reader of them! But what can I do? They are dictated to me. And if I rebel, it is only by inspiration of what is dictated. I flatter myself that I am escaping. Yet I find myself in the same spot from which I set out.

I continually find myself in the position of some flat creature that lives in a flat house and cannot imagine a curve. It walks about on the surface of a ball. It walks, flees, heads for the horizon. One day the flat creature sees ahead the house that it was fleeing and had left behind.

Le Potomak, La fin du Potomak, Opium, Essai de critique indirecte, just so many books in which I wandered on the edge of the void. This time, I'm tackling it head on. I'm scrutinizing it. I'm trying to catch it in treachery. "Search! Search!" a morbid game of hide-and-seek whispers in my ear. So speak those who have hidden something right before our very noses, and laugh at our clumsy attempts to find it. But I am determined. For we are sometimes able to fool those who would fool us. It seems to me that it is the poet's task to track down the unknown, and if the unknown should nab him—as it nabs Orpheus with the horse in my play, and with the Rolls in my film— Orpheus has thereby lost none of his connection to his own kingdom. He defies the invisible. He plays at he-who-loses-wins, while those who serve the visible can only play at he-who-wins-loses.

And all of these things—paintings, draw-ings, poems, plays, films—are made of carved-up time and space, a thick, folded wad of time and space. This wad is too thick to cut through. It shows only notches, cracks, and holes, all alien to one another. But within the folds, these holes, cracks, and notches are ar-ranged into a kind of lace, a geometry. Folded time and space would have to unfold themselves for us to see it. That is why I admire Picasso's frenzied need to carve up this wad, to unfold what can't be unfolded. A frenzy against surfaces. A frenzy that drives him to smash everything, make something new with the pieces, and smash this new something in his frenzy; to make files and use them to saw and twist the bars of his jail cell.

What can they understand of our rebellions, those people who think art is a luxury? Don't they know that we are in prison? Don't they know that our works are escaped convicts, and that because of this they are fired upon and loosed to the dogs?

And I am infuriated too, by my ink, by my pen, by my poor vocabulary in which I turn and turn like a squirrel that thinks it's running.

ON
TRANSLATIONS

On the train. *First Gentleman:* "Could you tell me the time?" *Second Gentleman:* "Tuesday." *Third Gentleman:* "Then this must be my station." It's not easy understanding one another.

In a Padua hotel, a tourist asks the concierge: "Could you tell me where I can find the Giottos?" Answer: "At the end of the hall, to the right." It's not easy understanding one another.

Were the Earth further than it is from the sun, it would still be unable to detect the sun's cooling, and the sun would continue to see us as a star. They would warm one another, without heat. It's not easy understanding one another.

It is particularly difficult understanding one another on this planet where languages erect impenetrable barriers between our works. And when works are able to penetrate these barriers, they climb up one side, and drop down the other disguised, so as to elude our police. Rarely do authors profit by such a climb.

It is not enough for translation to be a marriage. It must be a marriage of love. I am told that Mallarmé,

Proust, and Gide were fortunate in that regard. As for me, I came close to it with Rilke. But Rilke died just as he was beginning to translate *Orphée*.

There are translations of my work wandering about that are so crazy, one is compelled to wonder whether the translator has read me. In that case, to what must we ascribe the praise of foreigners? Perhaps it comes from a form of vapor that does not retain the bottle's shape, but exudes the living spirit of what it held. An Arabic genie, capable of carrying off a theater full of people.

The metamorphosis of a work through a language change suggests ideas that belonged to its original harmony, but do so no longer. On this coast, below Mount Agel, there is a jutting cape known as Dog's Head. It was once a Roman camp. The "tête de camp"—that is, the camp head—became "tête de can" in Nice patois—that is, Dog's Head. Today, everybody sees a dog's head in it. What do I know? Perhaps our translated works adopt silhouettes becoming to their legends. It is quite possible, just as it is possible for an atmosphere to alter outlines, that this is the very path that leads to glory.*

In the Jacobi-Goethe House, in Düsseldorf, at the supper which the town held in my honor, the mayor declared Goethe to be the great unknown of Germany. "He is venerated, which vitiates the requirement of reading him. He is so lofty that only his feet can be seen." Thus spake the mayor, and I deemed him to

---

* "See Naples and die"—in French, "Voir Naples et mourir"—should actually read "Voir Naples et les Maures"—that is, "See Naples and the Moors."

have spoken well. A work's prestige garners the kind of respect that forbade the Chinese from looking at their emperor. Looking at him, one became blind. Better to have been blind from the beginning.

In the final analysis, true glory begins when judgment ends, when the visible and the invisible become inextricable, when an audience applauds not the piece but its own idea of the piece, and itself for having had the idea. This sort of glory is appropriated by those theatrical actors who are unable to wait. Their shadow is not very strong, but it leaps into the light with all its might. They are compelled to do so by the immediacy of their servitude. Such was the acclaim received by Mme. Sarah Bernhardt—when she made her entrance, when she spoke, when she was silent, when she gesticulated, when she made her exit—that she was constrained to do more bowing than acting, and this acclaim was neither for her words nor her gestures, but for her ability merely to attempt such a thing at her age. The public was applauding its own refinement in understanding that the actress neither gesticulated nor spoke as her role demanded, but that she was performing a *tour de force* in its honor. It was congratulating itself on having this mythological creature washed up at its feet by the tides of fame, on being witness to this flesh-and-blood incarnation of the stories told by its parents and grandparents. One might also cite the case of the famous Russian singer who was able to reach the highest note on the register. At his final performance, all of St. Petersburg's high society gave him such an ovation when he opened his mouth to do his note, that no one ever knew if he had actually done it.

Let us return to our more modest glories. The journey undertaken by translated works is not commensurate with the pains we took to write them. That is as it should be. They are travellers, they grow weary of our hateful supervision. This is why I am careful never to complain. This is why I applaud the many German actresses who play in *La voix humaine*.[1] They serve up such bizarre texts that they tend to cry more than to cause tears. Which is a rather distressing sign that the tear-jerking machine is no longer working. We can certainly ascribe this to the progress of the guilty century in which we live. It would be silly to allow ourselves to be unduly affected by it. It was normal that writers should have been affected by it in eras when they believed their world to be both durable and attentive. As for me, I don't take it too seriously. I was born with open hands. Works and money slip through my fingers. Let those who would live by them, live by them. I'm happy just to write, since I cannot possibly shut up, nor become a mortal secret.

In any case, I find it remarkable that we can have any sort of communication with others. For they perceive only those parts of us that correspond to their level. The prompter for *L'aigle à deux têtes*[2] held forth endlessly on the beauty of Edwige Feuillère's feet. That is all the prompter could see of her from her pit.

When I look at the rushes of scenes shot the day before, I close myself off to specialists. Each one judges according to his own specialty. The cameraman according to the light, the gaffer according to his rails, the script-girl according to the positioning of the props, the actor according to his role. I remain the only judge.

Opinion is based on opinion. A precedent is required. Since no one dares to take the initiative, everyone watches everyone else. And, in any case, a tendency to mistrust one's own judgment would be more likely to drive an individual to express opinions contrary to his instincts. Caution stops him and (except in a town like ours, where evasive action is taken behind a volley of insults) inspires a respectful pause. This pause allows invisibility the time to pack its bags and flee before opinion is passed and the work is enveloped in a cloak of fallacy.

This is where individual translations begin. Their orchestra plays cacophonously. At the heart of this cacophony, the artist struggles to disentangle himself from the visible, while the invisible buries its gold.

The initial thrust must be strong enough so that something of the translated work remains at the end of the trajectory, and so that a foreign audience can recognize us in it. *L'aigle à deux têtes*, in an inaccurate adaptation, triumphed in London because of the leading lady. In New York, it flopped in an even more inaccurate adaptation, taken from the British adaptation by the actress who played the queen.

If we were miraculously to receive the gift of a new language, we would not be able to recognize the books we love. And if personal memories are connected to the errors in these translated works, and mingle with them, we would surely be sad to have lost them.

Occasionally, a book is steeped in shadow in its own country, while abroad it is brightly lit. Which goes to show that a work's invisibility carries more weight than its visibility.

We believe that our collaboration with our work should entail consequences. We flatter ourselves. It very soon has no need of our help. We were only its midwives.

Leonardo da Vinci was fortunate to be able to say almost everything in the international idiom of draughtsmanship. Explanatory drawings accompany his writings. His blackboard, streaked with chalk, often speaks to a class of uncultured pupils. But his chalk remains. It is translated through exegesis. That is what has happened to my 1930 film, *Le sang d'un poète*. The exegetes are translating it in America. They sometmes teach me about things I have put into it. Which in no way implies that I didn't put them there. On the contrary, for a layer of the film, invisible to me, belongs to the archaeologists who excavate the soul, uncovering the orders that directed my work without my suspecting their meaning. I finally come to realize this when I am interviewed, and my explanations are based on those of others. I had understood very little at the start. I saw only the visible. That is how work blinds us.

Exegeses come in all shapes and sizes. Some have taught me that the film paraphrases the life of Christ, that the snow in which the schoolboy's body is imprinted symbolizes Veronica's veil, and that I was led by the fact of the Eucharistical Congress' being held in Fontenoy to write the sentence: "While in the distance boomed the canons of Fontenoy." This exegesis came from an academic community where the young students read an obscene meaning into the factory chimney that can be seen tilting at the beginning and toppling at the end. To my knowledge, the chimney was merely intended to express the lack of passing time in this film, its events taking place while the chimney is falling. It remains true nonetheless that this and other exegeses troubled me, in the way that any affirmation can be disturbing.

Freud used to make rather awkward forays into my old film. Some declared it to be glacial and sexless. Others, to be sexually morbid. Here, then, is a visual work *translated into several languages*.

The fate of buried works is to be translated into several languages. Though it jeopardizes our own lucidity, invisibility has no objection to being excavated by others. This rather complicates the maze in which it conceals itself. Works that are too open attract nothing but tourists, who file past while distractedly consulting their catalogues.

Twenty years after *Le sang d'un poète*, the film

Orphée was translated into every language. I am speaking here of visual writing. The written word has been reduced to subtitles to which no serious person would attach the slightest importance. Germany has greatly educated me on the arcana of this film. Germany's deep attentiveness, its research, its philosophical, metaphysical, and metapsychical heritage, all prepare it well for excavations of this sort. A thousand letters from Germany submit, for my expert perusal, objects that have been dug up from my own soil. Objects still stained with lava and rust. And the gold stands out from the rest, in that neither lava nor rust have been able to blemish it.

Little by little, the archaeologists present my film to me in a way that I had never seen before, compelling me to account for it. There is in this an element of exchange that would grow sluggish were the work to remain untranslated.

To abandon the music of a sentence so as to communicate its rhythm alone. To leave this rhythm only an irregular pulse. To strip prose of its rhyme, because rhymes dull its edges, or to rhyme it purposely, blow upon blow. To shore up our rapidly leaking language with stacks of *which*'s and *what*'s. To plug it up with wads of ungrateful consonants, by syncopating overly long and overly short sentences. To sense that an upbeat or a downbeat (a masculine or a feminine gender) should precede a comma or a full stop. Never to lapse into the floral arrangements that people mistake for style; endlessly to do and undo (what might be called the Penelope Complex) . . . what becomes of these efforts to express myself, in a foreign idiom that we are satisfied can accommodate our ideas, when in fact it would be just as inconceivable to replace one physical body with another, and to expect it to inspire the same love.

I can translate a language more confidently if I know it badly. I have more difficulty with a newspaper article in German or English than with a poem by Shakespeare or Goethe. A great piece has its own contours, which my antennae can feel out in the manner of the blind reading Braille. Were I to know one of these languages too well, I would be disheartened by the impenetrable barrier of equivalences offered by a poem. Knowing it poorly, I can stroke it, prod it, squeeze it, sniff at it, turn it over and over. I can sense the landscape's least declivity. In the end, my mind rubs against these declivities like the needle of a gramophone. It is not the music contained within that emerges, but the complex shadow of that music. A complex shadow that conforms closely to its essence.

We must beware the translation of one of our texts if it seems fitting through its similarity to the original. It is like a mediocre portrait. One would prefer it to be subversive.

A method contrary to mine is perfectly defensible. The one is just as good as the other. There is often less risk when we are guided through a foreign language by one of our own countrymen. Our French language is rife with traps, with words having two spellings or two meanings (such as *trappe* and *chausse-trape*)†. Nothing is harder for a foreigner than to follow its caesuras and ellipses. Furthermore, there is my use of commonplaces in new contexts. Translated, my commonplaces become elegant stylizations. I was given proof of this with *La voix humaine* in England, where the commonplace sentence "il rôde comme une âme en peine"†† took on a Byronic lyricism.

The best thing is to let a work get on with it, from afar. It aspires to nothing but leisure. We might as well allow it to be happy, seeing how it scoffs at the care we continue to take on its behalf, and is irritated by it, like the son scolded by his mother, who notices neither that he is growing bigger, nor that he is growing uglier.

---

† "Trap" and "trapfall."
†† "He prowls like a soul in pain."

SIDETRACK

The invisible has its ways, and we have ours. It does not share our need to grow. It is happy just to abandon us. What does it care of our slavery, or of our fatuous insistence that we are free? We live only to serve it. The praise we garner through its operation is not ours to accept. We usurp its honors. We make off with titles and coats-of-arms that it allows us to steal, since they have nothing to do with its kingdom. Of what sort is this kingdom? I have no idea. Each day shows me that it is not mine, that I would be a fool to try to appropriate it. Which does not prevent me from being moved by the insults and praises I receive. Of that much I do confess, and blame myself alone. I am often ashamed of the privileges I arrogate, and having accepted, I resist them, when I should have resisted accepting them to begin with. My weakness won't allow it at the time they're offered. Afterwards, it's too late. In this way, my silence is an accomplice to the noise I abhor. My only saving grace is that I slip in my own misunderstanding amongst the others, that I overburden my disguise. Having been offered an exhibition of my paintings in Germany, I accepted out of fear of being put on show in France, while I should have exhibited neither my paintings nor myself anywhere at all. And notice how, in writing these lines, the delusion of responsibility makes me accede to the faults ascribed to me, pointing my slope in a direction it should not, and allowing me to believe that I am pointing it myself. For, from all the faults and weaknesses that I believe to be mitigated by my daring—which itself has been dictated to me—stem all those idiosyncracies that blend in with nature's handiwork.

That which is admired in the great masters, when they are passed through the sieve, could not exist without that which is condemned in them. The invisible brings them into the world by shackling them to a caricature of themselves, the burden of personality. This scam allows it to take hold, and to break out into the open. It draws the world's attention away from itself and onto its scapegoat, horns draped with medals and ribbons. For the invisible sinks its claws into that which is worst in us. It is there that it takes root, and thence that its tendrils creep. It could not do so without tasking us with that which it shirks, without weighing us down with scandal and success, with the addiction we have formed, and without which we would not be noticed. Its respect would make us superfluous, a vehicle sharing its privileges, a double, adding invisibility to the invisible, and giving it no room to spread its branches.

Invisibility is protected by the fact that we have taken its place as quarry, that we have learned to sit up and beg.

No sooner has it swindled us than it's already

dreaming up its next caper. In the meantime, it throws us into a thousand situations that serve its purposes and spite ours.

It knows very well that my understanding of the situation is irrelevant. Its next undertaking will find me dazed, disarmed.

This is where the poet's torment comes from, a torment he knows he's not responsible for, yet forces himself to believe he is, so as to give himself the backbone to suffer life until he dies.

Many poets have been unable to play the game. Some through suicide, some through drink, some through some sort of reclusion or escape, have managed to free themselves from their contract, all the more easily because they had served their time and the invisible no longer required their services. So it was that Rimbaud was helplessly crossing Paris in a cab with his sister at the very moment when Verlaine was beginning his famous article in the hospital. Rimbaud wanted nothing more to do with this city in which the invisible had milked him dry and, to punish his rebellion, was to pursue him all the way to Marseilles.

I still have no idea how I'm going to get out of it. Either I shall have to rid myself of the invisible, or it shall have to rid itself of me. These things are too tenebrous to broach. It's dangerous enough to go wandering off in the dark.

Until I was twenty, I believed that a poet could follow his fancy. All I got for my belief was foolishness.* Awaiting me at the end was a bath, and a cold one at that. For if the invisible takes us as its vehicle, it insists that we stick to our studies, which youth is loathe to do, preferring immediate gratification and success as its goals. My bath was followed by many years of austerity. Only age can teach us. Youthful arrogance prevents us from understanding this school for servants, and this master who allows us only to play the merry footman. Pranks that are punished with the rod.

I have noticed that the ethic which I built in order to be able to suffer this insufferable regimen has become contagious to those around me. It has been detrimental to some artists whose methods are ill-suited to patience and obscurity. With sadness, I distanced myself from them, so that they might no longer be made to suffer a rhythm that could only do them harm.

Here we have yet another chapter sidetracked down blind alleys. It's just the same when I am translated without any interference from the original work. Writing at my leisure, free from all constraint (or so I flatter myself), I tend to go astray. When translators in their turn go astray, this is their excuse as well. Nothing holds them back but professional conscience, which though weak remains a force, since it incites so many men to disobedience. To my mind, it is not strong enough unless we have an even stronger force living within us, condemning us to forced labor.

*I had published *La lampe d'Aladin*, *Le prince frivole*, *La danse de Sophocle*—three inanities.

ON
THE PREEMINENCE OF
FABLES

Man is utterly confused by the fact that a truth can be multiple, and each time we examine that which has been proffered as truth, we are surprised by the lack of correspondence between what we see and what we have been told about it. Our opinion is based on what is distorted within us and within others. Our readiness to mythify and to accept myth is incredible. A falsified truth very quickly becomes our gospel. We add our own two cents and, little by little, a picture is painted that bears no relation to the original.

Experience teaches us to beware this distorting faculty. Recently, at Villefranche, I allowed myself to be swept up in a fantasy, to wit: a ship on which a cruise cost ten million francs and carried only tourists draped in pearls, and to which I accepted an invitation, only to find a regular luxury liner, the same as any other, and on which a cruise cost a mere million, which is barely a dent in an American wallet. The passengers were in a class similar to that of pilgrims to

Rome, preachers, and honest little families, a far cry from the fairy tale that had been roundly described to me.

On this ship, I thought about how my own ideas on politics are based on what is peddled, and about governments that are as misinformed about our politics as we are about theirs. Great are the pains necessary to cure ourselves of such deceptive points of view. As it goes along, an anecdote changes dress, sex, size, age. It plods from mouth to mouth, from ear to ear. And it sometimes comes back to us so altered that we are unable to recognize it.

What is so serious about all this is that the transfigured picture of things takes on a life of its own. It replaces them in the compound of time and space, so that a painting will eclipse its model, which ceases to be credible. Man resents it for being unable to adapt to his mold, and for forcing him to take a new impression.

When an action unfolds, there are always variables that go unnoticed but which determine its uniqueness. It is this uniqueness that we find so striking, though we may only perceive it unconsciously. These are fairy tales in action, as many fairy tales as there are witnesses. Action takes on the presence of a work of art. It is fabulized through rhapsody, and through the troubadours who sing it from home to home. Thus does history evolve, and we would be greatly astonished if by some miracle we were allowed to spend one minute with Socrates or Alexander.

It is likely that the destruction of the Alexandrian Library, in which so many secrets were warehoused, cannot be attributed to the madness of a single leader, but that this leader was the tool of hidden forces that wished to impede knowledge, and to Return to Go.

Not a day goes by that I don't receive proof of those monsters born of our encounters. Our own legend should teach us about the inaccuracy that makes the world turn, and about the added threat this inaccuracy could pose as part of the ill will between nations, were this ill will not the result of a disorder willed by nature intent on producing the carrion on which she stuffs herself.

This is why, despite our will to resist them, fables seduce us. Their grip is too strong. We should see in this an echo of the universal rhythm. If all were in order between things, there would be dullness, which nature abhors.

When a government minister introduces an innovation into the system, the banks that were opposed to this minister and fought his program begin accusing him of willing their downfall, consider him an enemy to be overcome, which he soon is, and collaborate to preserve the briefly threatened imbalance. Fable soon begins to grow on the ruins of a monetary policy. Gold must take up its fallen crown. For tales of the Exchange are not the least of them. Fortunes rise and fall on mines, sugar cane, and oil wells that don't exist.

Radio allows us to catch one phenomenon of fabulation red-handed. This voice captures the speed of light and reaches us faster from a distance than it does listeners nearby, who hear it through the much slower speed of sound.

The night when the bells of liberation rang through Paris, I was visiting the household of Claude-Andre Puget, at the Palais-Royal, and we were able to listen to Jacques Maritain describing from New York that which we were concurrently experiencing. His spectacle looked nothing like ours. He had sublimated it and compelled us to believe. And he was right. New York had instantaneously substituted historical truth for our own. So it was too with the taking of the Bastille, which was much less than is told (less than that of the Tuileries), and of which Louis XVI was ignorant as he hunted hare on the site of what is now rue Mechain, near the boulevard Arago, the guillotine boulevard. We always celebrate the taking of the Bastille.

Unfortunately, if historical distortion tends to glorify, our personal distortion tends rather to disparage and vilify. I believe, however, that in the long run, this piling up of vilifying inaccuracies will elevate the plinth of one's memorial bust. A kind of truth can be discovered in them, particularly when inquisitive minds devote themselves to digging up the accuracies. The new fables which they uncover are added to the old, and eventually paint one's bust in beauiful colors.

If what every guest at a dinner table imagined about our souls were embodied in an object, we would be forced to take flight. We hang on through ignorance alone. The sudden discovery of the misapprehension that keeps us together would raze our pastures. There would be nowhere left for us to graze. There would be nothing left but to lie down and give up until death claimed us.

On the other hand, heartfelt companionship can put many things to rights. Yesterday three very old friends—myself among them—met after a long separation. Our ways of life and our works have nothing in common. Nevertheless, all three of us bathed in a liquor of friendship, much richer and more salubrious than any understanding born of shared habits and common turns of mind. The wife of one of my two friends said that our harmony stemmed from our threefold indifference to gossip, from the pleasure we took in our colleagues' success, from an inability to covet anything, and from having a gift for listening as strong as that for talking.

This liquor of friendship prevailed over our disparities, over the ideas we held of one another. As the conversation came round to our respective fables, one of us laughingly said that, in the end, they were caricatures of us, and that we should willingly recognize ourselves in them. He declared that I bring a certain acrobatic quality to the variations and modulations of my profile, and that it is fair that I be treated as an acrobat; that, being from Marseilles, he himself should be treated as a boules† player; and that the third amongst us should be treated as a newsstand writer, since his are the only books sold therein.

Our Marseillais did justice to his city's reputation.

---

†A game similar to the Italian *bocci,* played outdoors on a sandy pit.

We admired his mild acceptance of fables which, in terms of geography, are well-suited to his Marseillais temperament. He added that people would certainly be nonplussed to see us together, that they would see some sort of intrigue in it, while in fact our lengthy gossip session never once touched on other people's business, or on our work.

That same evening these friends wanted to drag me to a somewhat larger gathering. I refused to go, claiming that we would be sure to be sidetracked, and that I preferred not to break up the mood. And in fact, these larger gatherings do tend to degenerate into photography sessions and fodder for the gossip columns, such as the one in a Coast paper at the time that Sartre was finishing up *Le diable et le bon Dieu,* and I was beginning *Bacchus.* This column announced that we were collaborating on a play about Werther. Luther had become Werther. We later read an article in which it was thought fitting that our earlier undertakings had led us to study Werther's despair and suicide.

I believe that it is in *The School for Scandal* that a certain phrase, whispered at stage left, goes from mouth to mouth, and has become unrecognizable at stage right.

It is rare indeed that a person with whom we share a story does not stretch it out, embellish it, change its tack and its outcome. A story goes round, and it is just as common that, several years later, someone repeats it to us as if he had lived it himself. We are then constrained by civility to accept it as original.

Whistler had just told a good story at a supper at which Oscar Wilde was a guest. Wilde said he was sorry that the story wasn't his own, and Whistler told him: "It soon will be."

I've grown accustomed to people telling me, when I relate something I've seen, that I've made it up, or to reading words that are attributed to me but that I never said. For if the words are malevolent, the author accredits them to me, so that I draw the fire that he is glad to avoid. But such circuits are as nothing compared to the vast skein of inaccuracies in which the world is entangled. Clever indeed are they who can unravel it. We know that historical statements were never uttered. Who cares? They give character to figures who, without these statements, would remain indistinct and unrecognizable.

Eisenstein told me that scenes from his film *Potemkin* had become documentary photographs in the archives of the Russian Naval Department. His name had been dropped from them. When the film was being shown in Monte Carlo, he received a letter: "I was one of those sailors who was going to be shot under the tarpaulin." Now, Eisenstein had made up the tarpaulin incident, as he had made up the Odessa stairs where so many of his compatriots claim to have escaped the massacre. One is forever coming across fable that supersedes reality, the cake into which our daily bread is changed, by what means it is useless to try to foresee. Through what digestive tract. What becomes swollen and what becomes shrivelled. Mad indeed is the man who would attempt to build himself a fable and to convince the crowd of it. The same goes for anecdotes that spread despite their unknown origins. Each day a perfectly formed one appears, anonymously. They seem almost to be wafted about like pollen. Their aptitude for self-propagation is astounding. Likewise, those false reports that gallop along furiously, while we exhaust ourselves vainly trying to spread true ones. Likewise, a saying that passes instantly into public domain. De La Fontaine's are of that sort. Shakespeare's abound. This is what prompted an old Scottish lady, who had never read *Hamlet,* to say as she left Laurence Olivier's performance that the play was very nice, but had "too many quotations."

It is in fable that falsehood acquires noble rank. We should take care not to confuse it with idle gossip. There is a certain grandeur in its visions. Without them, we would not experience the charm of a Pegasus, or of the sirens, and a child could not preface a story about animals by telling me, "This was back when animals could still talk."

Nothing is more comical than that secure belief that our era (which, as Sartre points out, suffers from a bad conscience) represents an apex, and that it will never be laughed at in the way that it laughs at old movies. Youth can never picture itself as old, being questioned by youths who can make exactly the same mistakes, as they snicker and nudge each other and ask if it is true that people really got gas from pumps at the side of the road, if they really thought they were travelling fast, if they really danced in basements to the sound of the trumpet and the drum.

It is likely that science, which seems to us to reach to the very heart of things, will one day be dismissed as fable, and Einstein as just as much of a storyteller as Descartes, Erasistratus, or Empedocles.

Poetry probably has less chance of leading itself astray through its intuitive fables. Montaigne—who calls philosophy "sophisticated poetry"—is right to assert that Plato is just an "unstrung poet," and that if he can rise above the ridicule of having defined man as a "two-legged animal without feathers," it is only because he states that "Nature is but an enigmatic poetry."

He who would presume to resist fables would lose his skin to them. Fables have a very tough skin. They are the daughters of the invisible, the force it dispatches to spread confusion, a force well-trained to its task.

In my opinion, the mythologist is preferable to the historian. Once probed, Greek mythology is far more interesting than the distortions and simplifications of history, because its lies are in no way alloyed to reality, while history is an alloy of reality and falsehood. History's reality becomes a lie. The unreality of fables becomes truth. No falsehood is possible in myth, even if one argues over such and such a labor of Hercules, or whether he did them for love of Eurystheus or because he was in bondage.

We are hardly astonished at the sun's beseeching Hercules, or at its insisting Hercules promise not to shoot it with his arrows, to the point of lending him its golden chariot in which to cross the sea. We accept the funeral pyre, the blood- and sperm-soaked shirt given by Nessus to Deianira. We even grant that Hercules should dress as a woman and Omphale as a man.

Myth has knottier roots than history, and deeper ones. When we learn that the Danaides invented an irrigation system, it is truly marvelous to see this system developed as their torture.

The voyage of the Argonauts enthralls me more than any voyage of discovery to the Americas. My guess is that the Golden Fleece was none other than Medea's own hair, something that Jason and his friends were never able to understand. I am more fascinated by the crimes attributed to Medea—poisoning and bringing disaster—than by any doubt concerning the guilt or innocence of Catherine de Medici.

The most minor detail concerning Olympian families impassions us the way we are impassioned by Balzac's families, who have become real for us, or even those of *Fantomas*,† where the authors' negligence constantly gives Fandor a different father or mother. This has much in common with myth, and is what charmed both Apollinaire and myself about the book. The authors wrote us one day that they had a drawerful of less ridiculous manuscripts. We looked through

†The masked hero of a number of French novels written in the early twentieth century by Marcel Allain and Pierre Souvestre.

them. They were ridiculous, but the authors preferred them because of their realism.

In school, the history books stuff us with bland fables, while the legends of this entirely fabricated history invite us to discover its sources.

They are the very pinnacle of fable, and I marvel at their solemnity; for Hercules, having killed his master Linus with a sword-blow to the head, was acquitted by the tribunal because Linus had wanted to punish him and he had had the right to self-defense. Not a single hole in that magnificent purple fabric with which Greece wove an aristocracy of the invisible.

We should hail it as more truthful and intelligible than those troubled events whose unintelligibility is proven every day in the papers. Unless a Michelet,† or even an Alexandre Dumas, were to fabulize them.

The man who has developed a taste for fables can never sufficiently defend himself against their lascivious glance. As much foundation is needed in them as in earthly reality. Lao-tzu accused even Confucius of worldly frivolity. Leaving his house, Confucius told his disciples: "I have seen the dragon."

The famous stele of the child Septentrion who "danced for three days and died" does not commemorate a young Antibes dancer. It refers to the Mistral, a wind which blows for three days or for six. The in-

---

†Jules Michelet, 1798–1874. Leading French nationalist historian.

scription is a votive one, that of farmers who on the fourth day can finally return to work.

The severity of fables comes from the fact that all their branches grow from one seed. And since we have become fixated on Hercules, Augeas could have had no more than one filthy stable, so it was hardly necessary to divert the course of two rivers. If the washing had not become a Herculean labor, however, we would never have known the name of Augeas. Cerberus would have remained a mere guard dog lost by his master and found by Hercules, if Hercules had not had to go all the way to Hades to fetch him, and to promise Meleager's shade that he would marry her sister.

Chesterton was right when he wrote that Jerusalem is a little city with great ideas, whereas a great city has little ideas.

A square in Verona where fables are embodied is far more alive than any in which monuments are erected to the dead.

ON
A CAT STORY

To my knowledge, the cat story that was told by Keats has never been transcribed. It travels by word of mouth, changing as it goes. There are several versions of it, but its tone remains consistent. Such is the subtlety of this tone, that I am led to wonder if it doesn't explain why this story is better suited to the spoken word and its hesitations, than to the hasty pen.

Here are the facts. Keats was expected in the village of F., where he was to dine with his friend, the rector. There was a forest to be crossed. Riding through this forest, Keats lost his way. The falling night made the maze inextricable. Keats decided to wait for the dawn, to tether his horse to a branch, to seek out some woodcutter who might have a cabin and could offer him shelter until daybreak.

As he wandered, never quite daring to lose sight of his horse, and taking care to mark the tree trunks that he might find his way back, he perceived a light.

He made his way toward this light. It was coming from a sort of ruin, the likes of which are not to be

found in any travel guide. It was an ancient amphitheater, a coliseum, a tangle of arches, of terraces, of
crumbling stone, sections of wall, nooks and crannies,
undergrowth.

The weird light flickered and brought the dead
circus to life. Keats drew nearer, slid behind a column,
and peered through one of the cracks.

He was frozen with astonishment and fear by
what he saw. The amphitheater was overrun by hun-
dreds of cats, taking their places one next to the other,
like the crowd in the arenas of Spain. They milled
about and howled. Suddenly, the sound of tiny clar-
ions was heard. The cats stood still, turning their
glowing eyes to the right, toward the source of the
dancing light and shadows. The lights were emanat-
ing from torches that were carried by fifty cats in
boots. These cats were followed by a procession of cats
dressed in magnificent costumes, pages and heralds
playing trumpets, cats bearing coats-of-arms and cats
bearing standards.

The procession crossed the track and skirted
round its edge. There appeared four white cats and
four black cats, bearing swords and felt hats and, like
all the other members of the procession, walking on
their hind legs, and carrying on their shoulders a little
coffin, on top of which rested a little golden crown.
Two by two, there followed cats carrying cushions,
with embroidered diamond crests that glinted under
the torchlight and moonlight. Drummers brought up
the rear of the procession.

Keats thought, "I am dreaming. I have fallen
asleep on my horse and I am dreaming." But dream is

one thing and reality is another. He was not dreaming; he knew it. He was lost in a forest by night and was attending a ritual not intended for the eyes of men. He was frightened. Once his presence was discovered, this horde of cats would flock from the circus and tear him to bits with their claws. He withdrew further into the shadows. The heralds sounded, the standards waved, the coffin was paraded about, and all this in a silence that was enhanced by the proud little trumpets.

Having completed a full circuit of the track, the procession moved on. The trumpets were silenced. The lights went out. The crowd of cats left the terraces of the amphitheater. A number of cats leapt through the fissure against which Keats flattened himself so as to be invisible. The ruin became once again a ruin, overrun by the light of the moon.

It was then that an idea welled up within Keats that was more dangerous yet than the spectacle he had just witnessed. *He would not be believed.* He would never be able to relate his story. It would be taken for a poetic lie. Now, Keats knew that poets do not lie. They bear witness. And Keats also knew that they are commonly believed to lie. And Keats was maddened by the thought that such a secret would remain his own, that he could never relieve himself of it, or share it with his peers. It was a catafalque of solitude.

He shook himself, found his horse, and made up his mind to leave the forest at any cost. This he managed to do, and he arrived at the presbytery, where the rector was no longer waiting up for him.

On a Cat Story

This rector was a highly cultivated man; Keats respected him and believed him capable of understanding his poems. He told him his story, without alluding to the circus of cats. The rector had gone to bed and arisen again. The servant slept, so the rector set the table. Keats ate in silence. The rector was astonished at his distracted manner. He asked him whether he were sick. Keats answered that he was not, but that he labored under a disquietude the cause of which he was unable to divulge. The rector gently pressed him and urged him to explain himself. Keats turned away, shut himself off. At length, the rector achieved a certain headway, his guest having declared that his unrest stemmed from the fear of not being believed. The rector promised to believe him. Keats demanded more. He begged the rector to swear on the Bible. This the rector could not do. He asserted that his promise as a friend was equal to his oath as a minister. "I'm all ears," he said, leaning back into his armchair and smoking his pipe.

Keats was about to speak when he bethought himself. Fear seized him again. It was necessary for the puzzled rector to allow him the freedom of silence in order to loosen his tongue.

Keats closed his eyes and gave forth. The rector listened from the shadows. The stars shone through the open window. The fire crackled. Before the hearth, the cat appeared to doze. Keats described the ruins, and the strange spectators of the strange spectacle. From time to time he would open one eye, throwing a glance at the minister who, eyes shut, drew on his pipe.

The thing happened like a crash of thunder, so that neither of the two men was able to grasp it, or to give an exact account of what was going on.

Keats had reached the procession, the torches, the trumpets, the banners, the drums. He was depicting the costumes, the felt hats, and the boots. "Four white cats," he was saying, "and four black cats were carrying a coffin on their shoulders. On top of the coffin was a golden crown."

No sooner had he uttered these words than the cat, which had been sleeping by the fire, drew itself up into a bowed arch, its fur bristling, and cried out in a human voice, "But that means I am King of the Cats," and leapt out the window.

ON
MEMORY

If the contents of our memory were able to materialize and roam about, they would clutter up the entire world. How amazing, then, that such a clutter can fit into our brain. All the more so, since young memories are of such weak constitution that they stumble, while the old ones are of such strapping constitution that they trample all over the young. When we come across an old one, it drags with it the clod of soil from which we have ripped it. Which is why I am always reluctant to write my memoirs— memoirs in which the dates would get all confused and jumbled, in such a way that my perspectives would grow lame and unable to stand on their own.

In dream, false perspectives are analogous to those dictated by art.* Memory flaunts our rule within it. People dead and alive move about on an artificial

---

*The instantaneous nature of dream is such that one can dream in the space of a second the equivalent of Marcel Proust's entire work. For that matter, Proust's work is closer to dream than what is commonly passed off as dream narrative. It has the innumerable cast, the shifting plots, the lack of chronological sequence, the cruelty, the dread, the comical, the precise set design, even the "all's-well-that-ends-badly."

stage, lit by fatal lighting. Memory is free. It com-
poses. It compiles. It compounds. It offers us spectacles of an order of truth higher than any realm that
simply obeys the strictures of our limitations. It strips
us of our limitations and overthrows chronology. Our
neurons float like seaweed in the water of the night,
touching one another, beyond our control. We live a
life unconstrained by the rails we travel on. Control
snaps on upon awakening. Memory puts its equipment away, and grudgingly allows us the use of but
the barest essentials.

As for me, there is a great amount of ill will in our
relationship. When it listens to me at all, it answers by
subterfuge or surprise, as when, for instance, a name
eludes me, and I harry my memory until it throws me
the name like a bone, just so I won't bother it any-
more.

I don't know which philosopher it was that
said: "We are walking on Roman rooftops." That is
just how we felt in Alexandria, where the new city is
built on top of the old.*

---

*The Egyptologists' dispute illustrates the disrepute into which
certain kinds of research have fallen. The accidental death on a
French highway of Alexandre Varille, the best of our young Egyptologists, is an example of the defense put up by the unknown at
every level. The official Egyptologists' capricious mockery of Varille's
work *L'escalier est dans la concierge* hardly decides the issue, the
stairway being as much in the concierge as the concierge is in the
stairway. My concierge proved this to me by refusing to bring up my
mail, saying that it was pointless since there was going to be a war. In
this case, the stairway was indeed in the concierge, and prevented
her from climbing the stairs.

It floats there like a memory. One detects its presence like some phantom recollection, when we feel it to be there without being able to respond to our queries. Wasn't Nero's four-thousand-room palace buried under a man-made hill on which the baths were subsequently built? And hadn't Rome *forgotten* this palace, until the day a hole caved in and Michelangelo broke his leg on a *memory*? To be precise, the memory was the Laocoön group that decorated the ceiling.

Entire periods of our lives are buried away. One little hole, one name that I bump up against, is enough to awaken four thousand rooms, and a thousand walking, talking statues with it.

The Egyptian king Tutankhamen's tomb was a kind of memory, in that his everyday appurtenances were piled up, dislocated, squeezed in, bricked up, inextricably, and unexplainably, in a tiny cellar, in which, as a dead man, he was expected to restore them for his own use, without disturbing the mess.

It was impossible to enter this cellar. It took ten years for these remembered objects to take form and to embellish an entire floor of the Cairo Museum, whence my memory dispatches them to me.

Egyptologists are forced to wonder whether these objects may be replicas, and whether those that have come to us were the ones which the Pharoah used, or were copies made for his tomb.

One is forced to wonder whether the recollection of a dream is not composed of replicated objects that memory allows us, while keeping the originals for itself. And in fact, when someone tells you his dream, he seems to describe settings, players, and actions that have as much in common with the dream's settings, players, and actions as an actor dressed up as a statesman has in common with that statesman. Recalled dreams are so far removed from their original lighting and effectiveness that they bore those who are told about them, and who did not attend the show. They wilt. They lose their sheen like an aquatic plant out of water.

When we close our eyes and ask memory to dredge up an event that occurred in a room in which we are standing, memory sends us a different one, similar yet situated elsewhere. In the same way, when we awaken abruptly in a hotel room in which we are stopping on our way home from the country, we must take care not to get up too fast if we want to reach the toilet. For memory will send us our room in the country, so that we will look for the door there where it is not, and injure ourselves against the furniture. Memory delights in the sight of our losing and injuring ourselves. Memory also delights in sending us one of its own personal spectacles as one of ours, allowing us to believe that a scene from a dream is actually from our real world.

I could write volumes on this subject. This awful storehouse frequently victimizes me with its switches and swindles. The problem is, I would have to apply in the exact place where I am being cheated, and they would probably enlighten me only so as to cheat me further.

On Memory

Some people who complain about their memory find it more obedient after a traumatism. (The retention of numbers, for instance, can be greatly enhanced by a trepanation). This very thing happened to Matisse, who had absolutely no memory for numbers until, coming out of sedation, he found it at his fingertips.

The storehouse of memory is not at my disposal. I have the greatest difficulty in getting anything out of it. And when I do, I repeat, it is only condescendingly granted me. The prop supplied by the shadows raises a cloud of dust that vaguely resembles the period that surrounded it. It is in this manner that I manage to relive certain periods, with the help of a detail that memory deigns to provide. This detail falls back into the shadows the moment I have noted it, and will reappear only in my dreams, in which memory, a miser no longer, opens wide the storehouse door. It seems that sleep is its kingdom, that with neither passport nor papers it furnishes the players, the scenery, and the props necessary to its productions, and to which we are, each of us, a Louis II of Bavaria—the sole spectator. It offers us these shows, yet seems to balk at furnishing us with the necessaries to produce our own, and at leaking its material to the outside world.

This bureaucratic remoteness affected by memory, this haughty indifference to what is politely inquired, has gradually discouraged me from its box office. I have learned to be satisfied with stockpiling it with the present—which ceases to be so as it passes from sight. Let memory file it, classify it, catalogue it, what do I care! This present reverts to the twilight to which I myself will someday revert, and of which only fragmentary images will be drawn from me. For stockpiling the warehouse of memory can have deleterious effects on what is stockpiled. And what I retrieve is not always in one piece. A name, a face, an event— such things are damaged beneath the piles of junk. Often all I can manage is a harvest of scrap, and I exhaust myself only to learn that the rest of it can't be found or no longer exists.

The phenomenon of memory invites us to the marriage of time and space, a marriage that begets the faulty perspective that distorts our vision, that allows us to advance in one direction only, while we retreat in the other only with the help of that faculty. Sleep dissolves that mirage and unveils a world seen without our blinkers, in which we would finally come to see that our so-called human freedom is that of a pack horse. But man hates to be minimized. He even fears poetry since it began scrawling insults on our dungeon walls. Freud's *Interpretation of Dreams* gives poetry some consolation in that the obscene graffiti with which it covers the walls are everyday sights to the human eye.

My memory is never so happy as when I ignore it. I thus leave it free to set up a show for the following evening, to rehearse it, to arrange the lighting, without any interference on my part. I do not know the relationship of its inner twilight to the one that issues me my orders. Whether they are compatible or incompatible. Whether it is just as hatefully casual. Whether they are in league together. I am rather inclined to believe that certain recollections are in my own pocket, that they come from elsewhere, somewhere alien to the work that is compelled of me—work that authorizes them only when it can profit by them.

When memory dozes it keeps one eye open, so I am wary of its tricks. It releases some absurd article from storage, and imposes it upon us. Usually, the imposed article is of a painful, aggressive absurdity. Does memory impose it simply as a display of power? And indeed, try as we might to ignore it, to send it back where it came from, memory shoves it into our faces. Memory seems to revel in the discomfort the article provokes, pumping it up and magnifying it until it blocks our sunlight. Some people reap a bitter satisfaction from this. Spleen and depression feast on it. But that's not my style. I would prefer that the gloomy warehouse dispatch nothing but pleasant articles my way. The strength of my childhood memories consoles me for my lack of control over it. They fear the night, they disobey, they fling open the doors, reaching me out of breath, their cheeks burning. It is true that they are soon obliged to leave me, to melt back into the shadows. My *Portraits-souvenirs*[1] bore them witness. Memory seemed powerless to restrain them. They escaped in droves. It would not be the same thing to call up more recent recollections. Then we would have to resume all the waiting, the paperwork, the interviews attendant upon a discourteous bureaucracy. It is for this reason that I have abandoned the attempt, despite the offers I have received from many sources.

The only thing I stand to gain from this bureaucracy is that many bad memories are lost in it. One might even say they are discarded. On the other hand, it preserves many an insignificant recollection that might be compared to a lace curtain that is spared in a conflagration. Such recollections, which memory undervalues and fails to lock away, are readily disposed of. Memory has no idea that those are my favorite kind, and that they refresh my heart.

The storehouses of memory do not hold only our own articles. They also hold those of our fathers and our fathers' fathers. This mitigates the disorder and the ill-humor of its searches.

Memory's bureaucracy will sometimes mix up its requisitions as well, and show us a new episode as if we had already lived it. This phenomenon lasts but a split second, and occurs very rarely. The mistaken requisition is betrayed by the insignificance of the episodes that memory shows us, as if it were retrieving them from within before having ever inserted them there.

Memory often delivers the requisitioned article out of context, that is, without a second article that would make it fit for use. For example, it may deliver a face without the name that goes with it, or a name without the face that personifies it. Or it won't deliver a familiar name precisely at the moment when we need it to introduce one person to another. It leaves us open-mouthed when that person notices our dismay, asks us if we recognize him, then requires us to show that we do, particularly when we are quite certain of having recognized him and only his name eludes us.

Our inability to obtain a particular article does not prevent us from becoming aware of the empty space that it should fill, and by which we perceive its shape while being unable to identify it. This empty space is as distinct as the white rectangle left by a painting removed from a dirty wall, or the impression of a jewel on the velvet of an old display case. Velvet and wall bear witness to an absence which they can neither name nor describe. Such is the trickery of memory's bureaucracy, that it is more ready to dispatch us the wall and the velvet than the painting or the jewel. And I am not speaking here of a design without an artist, a word without a mouth, a place without geographical references. I am speaking of the shape of emptiness, an emptiness having shape, an emptiness in a void, an emptiness that tortures us because it outlines that which should be, yet the phantom article refuses to name itself.

I am avoiding any discussion of such mundane phenomena as pentothal, hypnosis, and psychoanalysis. The storehouse of memory has little respect for these artificial means of ambush. It releases but little, barely surpassing the amount that it would release without connivance. Even if it is just playing around, and releases articles requisitioned by falsehood. So it is that husbands, having insisted on attending the pentothal experiment, have heard their wives confessing indiscretions they did not commit and depravities of which they were innocent. You may rejoin that it was within them because they should have liked to have been guilty of these depravities and to have committed these indiscretions. But that has nothing to do with memory. Such articles come from a different stock.

The *Mémorial de Sainte-Hélène* documents for us the management of memory's bureaucracy. The Emperor continually asks Las Cases why he had not been informed earlier on such or such a reform. Las Cases fills out a requisition, from which he dredges up memories of an unapproachable, inaccessible emperor, deaf to his counsellors' advice. Isolated with Las Cases, the Emperor can no longer imagine a Las Cases for whom it was impossible to meet and speak with him.

Certain ruins are so deeply impregnated with ideas and events that memory seems to live within them, helping them to survive. This is particularly striking at the Parthenon, which I approached in 1936, full of scholarly suspicion. I arrived at midday, in the middle of an implacable silence. The first thing that struck me was the fact that this silence could speak. It spoke an unintelligible language, but speak it did. And I became aware that this informal language was coming from the columns. A pink flame lives yet within them. They spit it out in exchange for memories.

Other columns are dead, and speak only through our mediation, such as those at Sunium, whose temple is a skeleton eaten away by sea salt. They rise up like the ashes of erect cigars. They are silent. Despite the loudspeakers that surrounded them in 1949 and lent them a sort of oracular organ. Lord Byron's signature there barely raises a cricket's chirp. But compared with the ruins of the Athenian Acropolis, the ruins at Cape Sunium have no memory.

How I digress! I, who wanted to be worthy of the scholar to whom I dedicate these notes. That is impossible. I offer him my apologies. Too many contradictions must jump out at him, though he himself is an expert on the theory of opposites, and assures me that poets find first, only to seek afterwards.

How I would enjoy piecing well-cut stones together and building from them a temple dedicated to Minerva! A temple in which I need no longer fear her fierce, blue-eyed helmet, resembling the number 7. But instead I blindly pile up boulders of unreason. I surrender myself to the bliss of disobedience. I wallow in it. From time to time my disobedience wearies me, and then I obey. Perhaps my periods of obedience will shed light on the others, will leave their mark on my boulders of unreason, as one finds dates on those of the Eleusinian chaos.

My ideal would have been to have a writing table at which I could sit at scheduled hours. To find the appropriate words for discourse. To lead this discourse at my leisure. Not to lose myself in its margins. Not to lose my sense of direction. To find my way by the stars.

None of this is within my power. I aspire to it without understanding it, and will never understand it.

Alas, why do I not have your muted lamp, my dear René, or your firm grip, my dear Sartre, to guide my descent into my night? Why can't poets be what they should be: teachers. A thousand superstitions shackle the poet. In Sartre, the total absence of superstition. He walks under every ladder.

With his *Saint Genet*[2] (the preface to the *Complete Works* of Jean Genet) we see this process: over the space of five hundred seventy-three pages, wearing a linen mask and a surgeon's white robe, Sartre opens up Genet on the operating table. He disassembles the machinery. He puts it back together again. He sews him up. Genet breathes free. He will have no pain when he awakens. But when Genet rises from the operating table, he will leave another Genet behind, who will rise in his turn. One will have to conform to the other, or take flight.

In a dream Sorbonne, Sartre has improvised a monstrous thesis which none of his colleagues would dare to attempt. On the checkerboard of our timid era, he pushes his chessmen so far that the game is blocked. He wins. I lose. I shove my pieces about in a panic, and the slightest breeze snuffs out my lamp.

P.S. In my book *Opium* I have discovered an instance in which memory can be induced to put forth its material by one particular sign, where it would not by another. A sort of "open sesame."

One day on my way to rue Henner, I passed rue La Bruyère where I spent my youth at no. 45, a town house in which my grandparents had occupied the second floor, and we the mezzanine (the ground floor being but a study hall open to the courtyard and trees of the *Jardin Pleyel*). I decided to overcome that fear which habitually causes me to run down that street with my eyes closed and my ears stopped. The carriage gateway being ajar, I stepped through beneath the archway.

I was looking with great surprise at the trees of the courtyard where my summers had been divided between my bicycle and making puppets, when a suspicious concierge stuck her head out of a skylight that had once been boarded up, and asked me what I was doing there. I told her that I was having a look around my childhood home, to which she replied: "You don't say," left the skylight, joined me in the lobby, looked me over, would allow herself to be swayed by no argument, practically threw me out, and slammed the gate behind me, raising with this sound of distant cannons a host of new memories. After this failure, I had the idea of running down the street with my eyes closed, from the rue Blanche to no. 45, dragging my right hand along the surface of the buildings and the street lamps, as I had used to do on my way home from school. The experiment not yielding a great deal, I realized that in those days I had been much shorter, and that my hand was now at a higher level, so that it was not passing over the same contours. I repeated the stratagem. Thanks to the mere change in height—and by a phenomenon analogous to the running of a needle along the grooves of a gramophone record—I coaxed forth the music of memory. Everything came back to me: my cloak, the leather of my satchel, the name of the friend who walked with me, those of my teachers, certain things I said, the tone of my grandfather's voice, the smell of his beard, and even of my sister's and mother's sewing fabrics.

ON
DISTANCES

M. Langevin: *"But how do you measure these things?"*
Einstein: *"These things cannot be measured."*

COLLÈGE DE FRANCE, 1923

Our senses limit us to being within two points. The musical scale provides us with an example of such limitation. Like it or not, we have to live with it. Certain plants, certain types of gas, can sometimes stretch us in one direction or another. (Peyote raises us above our scheme of perspective and color. Nitrous oxide raises us above our scheme of time). And dream itself allows us in one second to live through plots as thick as Marcel Proust's.

But our disobedience to the rules could certainly be a richer disobedience than merely overcoming fatigue and staying up late, instead of obeying with the tender discipline of morning glories that curl up, change color, and fall asleep as soon as night falls. A thousand avenues of disobedience are open to us. A thousand files with which to saw at our cell bars. A thousand knotted ropes to climb down—at the risk of breaking our necks. Is it not the prisoner's obsession to escape, even with some guard firing upon us, recapturing us when we reach the ground, and salting us away into our cells again?

Well may you whip the sea like Xerxes, throw down a challenge to Mount Athos, or like the Thracians fire arrows at the sky—you will have changed nothing. Far wiser is it to grapple with kingdoms that will not make us ashamed of our actions, because our actions will go unscrutinized.

The glory of painters (gained in opposition to the tribunal that first judges them) stems from their transgression of the aesthetic laws that box them in, from their smashing of that box and their imposition of an order that is generally seen as disorder, and with which they replace the most recently established order.

It was in musing on this canvas and its ineluctable colors—against which they furiously batter their heads, like insects against a window—that I had the idea of seeking freedom on paper, for better or for worse, of developing a theory of distances, a theory to the effluvia of which I myself am subject, and from which my only escape lies in its definition and expulsion from myself. An impregnable theory, since man's only defenses against it are primitive, no matter how ultimately perfected he may believe them to be.

Proust was unquestionably able to perceive real time, its affectation of illusory perspectives, and ourpotential for imposing new ones upon it. But

Proust's anchors are too heavy. His overweaning gluttony anchors him too strongly to a wild rose, a hotel table, a particle, a dress, for him ever to be truly able to take flight.* It may well be legitimate in his case, since his only goal is the defeat of realism. Glued, he says, to the sensation of immediacy, he falls into another kind of realism that he restricts to a montage of aural and visual snapshots reconstructed by a distorting function of memory.

It is therefore a novelist's technique that he advocates, and to good effect. Which is not to say that one can't seek other avenues of escape, since the potential for this sort of experiment is boundless. It is to man's credit that he is able to imagine that which has no image, which does not make it any easier to name the unnameable, particularly when we lack a scientific vocabulary. In short, the stuff of which we are made is far more distant from us than any observable galaxy. It is inobservable. Too far (too close) to be so. Subject to a distancing mechanism that eludes us.

Is there any real distinction between heavy and light, thick and fast, large and small, or any other

---

*Proust's three praxes: To desire things from afar; not to take pleasure in them when once he has them; to break from them so as to be able to take pleasure in them from afar.
This "afar" being his "anear," nearness distances him from things to the point where they become invisible. *Example:*

> But above all, the diminution of pleasure which I had previously attributed to the certainty that it could never again be taken from me . . .
> That evening, the belief, and the subsequent evaporation of the belief that I was going to meet Albertine, had within the space of a few seconds rendered her in my eyes almost insignificant at first, then infinitely precious.

certainties amongst the less certain? We write laws based on our own infirmities, yet we refuse to admit that they may not be universal and that, as often happens between two nations, their only value is the one that their makers assign to them. The evidence suggests to me that our legislation would be found puzzling across certain borders, that this legislation may be applicable only to our republic (of which the chemists, mathematicians, historians, astronomers, philosophers, and biologists are the legislators), and that if we are not free to express our certainty of the truth, we are certainly free to presage it.*

It is within this borderline between the visible and the invisible that everything exists, and upon it that everything wavers, so that anything that approaches it does not shrink, yet somehow remains small. And (human) smallness, between what interests me (insects, microbes, neutrons, electrons), and what doesn't (the wholly imperceptible): the borderline is diffuse and indistinct, and thereby all the more alien. On the one hand, scales of value, size, weight, and volume; on the other, a scale that eludes us because of that near yet impregnable distance which I have made the topic of my research.

We should take it to its logical conclusion, and say that if there is neither weight nor volume, nor can

---

*There are mathematical prodigies. Evariste Galois, the Rimbaud of mathematics, dead on May 19, 1832 at the age of 20, killed by pedagogues after having written sixty pages that continue to this day to reveal unexplored perspectives to scientists. "I am a barbarian," he said, "because I am not understood." And: "I have completed research projects that will stop many a scholar in his."

there be distance, and that not only do distances fool us, they are also the result of a defensive malfunction of our machinery. Just as we had decided (believed to have ascertained) that there were heavy things and light things, large things and small things, so did we establish that there were near things and far things; if we find this convenient in one way, we find it bothersome in another, for it prevents us from following the path that would free us from our cell, and would allow us to leave it without leaving it.

In such realms, how marvelous it would be to treat distance the way we treat the alphabet when, despite the distance that separates A from Z, we form words like "azure" or "Zamora," simply by suppressing alphabetical distance.

Instead of "how small it is," we would have to get used to saying "how far it is," and to believing it, sensing that the distance exists when it does not appear to, that the fact of taking something in our hand, and of the hand itself, are at immeasurable distances from our thought and vision. We would then be able to imagine a hidden scale that would allow us, not to see the invisible, but to avoid situating it in another kingdom.

A form of distance as yet unknown lets us believe that what is near cannot be far. Such an error blinds us to the planetary machinery, in which the infinitely large and the infinitely small are not spread out as on a spectrum, but coexist as one model that fools us by sleight-of-hand, by blinkering our senses, by a secret law of relationships.

For this remoteness has nothing to do with that from which we are distancing ourselves. It makes the near imperceptible, and blinds us, for instance, to the nature of the matter that surrounds us, both invisible and visible to our eyes. It hides entire worlds from us, and worlds within worlds whose enigmatic remoteness makes them appear as one dense mass, and it makes us believe this fable to be true. It weaves an illusory appearance around every last object.

We are able to recognize the contour and size differences in an image only by a mental process that we assume to be instinctive, but that in actual fact is not. Eisenstein told me how, during the filming of *The General Line,* he had wandered into an *izba.*† Two postcards hung on the wall. One was of Cléo de Mérode, the other, of the Eiffel Tower. To his questions, the old peasant woman whose room this was answered that they were the emperor and the empress. She was aware neither of the new regime, nor of what was depicted in the pictures. For her, pictures could only be those of the tsarina and the tsar.

Certain Indians of the high mountains, where there are neither mirrors nor lakes, were able to recognize other natives in a group photograph, but were unable to recognize themselves, asking after the strangers' identity. At least they were able to read the picture, while many tribes cannot and look at it upside-down.

†A small Russian country house (vacation home).

This mental process is as difficult to accomplish regarding a realist image as it is a cubist or abstract one. The mind is accustomed to a focusing whereby the realist image is instantly translated. It has not yet learned to focus images that speak to the mind's eye.

What is there to say about our focus on temporal and spatial perspectives, concerning which men have only the most delusory and muddled notions! To such an extent that, finding myself in a hotel in which I have not been for several years, I am soon believing that I never left it, and the shape of the place somehow wipes away the intervening time between my two stays.

Man comforts himself with a conception of the present that is as false as a reflection in running water. But the water of flowing time determines the aging of the stationary image it reflects. This image, then, though stationary, flows in a manner different from the water of time, which flows without carrying away the reflection. It is because neither is the reflection stationary, nor does the water of time flow, and the whole thing regulates itself according to rules that remain elusive to us.

It has become a sort of boldness these days to imagine that the tiniest microbe might contain a whole horde of them, and so on. A doctor would hardly dare to suggest, in 1952, that he has discovered a tiny microbe containing one single, tinier microbe within it. What if that doctor should guess—and if we should, too—that that particular form of invisibility is still connected to our kingdom, and that there is yet another connected to laws of which our senses can't even conceive! And yet I believe the microbe is not small, since it does not appear so to itself, and that even within our own kingdom this monster is not small, but *far*. Such remoteness is astonishing. We would be far more amazed, however, should the real remoteness, which eludes our kingdom and extends past the frontiers of understanding, reveal itself.

Alas! I lack the professorial ease that would allow me to pursue this line of research.

But there is nothing to say that artificial senses may not one day expand the field of investigation of our own, and that my blind man's cane may not come across the reality of da Vinci's discoveries or of Verne's phantasms.

It is likely that nothing has an ending or a beginning. Once the idea of the minute has been rejected, one must accept that there are worlds upon worlds swarming in all those directions that we designate as vast or small; that all of these worlds are equally voluminous (except as regards such explosive and fragmentary systems as our own); and that it is only our inability to imagine this that incites us to populate the vastness with gods and to believe that the infinitely small is limited.

It is therefore a certainty that a new conception of distance would abolish the ridiculous notion that nothing can be *infinitely* small, and that, drained of meaning, the concept of large and small would save us from losing our way and bumping up against the phantom ramparts of the vast and the minute.

Since any communication is already close to impossible, nothing is harder to communicate to others than this idea of the infinitely small without bounds, while the idea of the infinitely large without bounds gains from the sort of amorphousness that appeals to so many accommodating minds. It is impossible to get someone to admit that the image of his portrait on a magazine cover, in which he is shown holding the same magazine, can diminish to imperceptibility, but need not and does not stop there or anywhere. In contrast, it is easy to get him to acknowledge his own glorious body, and the apotheosis in which this glorious body takes part. The idea of such a dead point, from which a sort of endless funnel extends itself, is hardly rational, but it does bring solace to reason. Such solace allows one to avoid superfluous discomfort, as well as any research that would negate other research believed to have been established once and for all.

When we are told that an electron weighs one millionth of a milligram, it does not mean that it weighs any less than a planet. Yet again, it is our perspective on this unknown distance that deceives us concerning their respective weights. A mental illusion, just as there are optical illusions.

What determined me to write this book after *La difficulté d'être*[1] was that I was writing for that endangered species of people who *read* instead of reading *themselves,* and who give careful scrutiny to the author's terminology. People tend to slip on words, and not to understand that the manner in which they overlap is an indispensable element of their expression. A sentence's meaning is not the be-all and end-all. It is the essence that counts. The intimate meaning can only stem from the painting style, and not from what the canvas depicts.

If the meaning of words is disrupted, what will become of their essence? Yesterday, we heard a lady repeat the word "obfusted" several times, when she meant "obfuscated," without realizing that people were laughing at her. Just this morning, another lady was amazed to learn that the sea had salt in it. I have noticed that those who deride such ladies are themselves taken by surprise when face to face with similarly obvious facts; but in a realm (our own) on which it may be thought improper to dwell. "It is not in the curriculum"—our students' excuse for their own idleness.

There are several kinds of distances that do not resemble distance as registered by our senses. Seen atomically, our system's time-scale is so dizzying (the telescope being a mere corrective lens, and the microscope cheating us with close-up views of that which never ceases to be remote) that its details disappear like the blades of a fan. Seen from yet another distance, this whirlwind freezes, forming an integrated block of past, present, and future. Eternity is another term based on our conception of time, and no more than time, eternity is inconceivable. By this I mean that its meaning is lazily applied. Within the word "always" is a concept of continuity contrasting with the static phenomenon that short-lived humanity replaces with the illusion of duration. Which is why I once wrote, without being too expansive, that time is a phenomenon of perspective analogous to Holbein's death's-head. We should therefore come up with a word expressive of neither flowing nor stasis, and such a word is impossible to come up with since words refer to a convention which is eluded by that *thing* without being. It is the opposite of nothingness. The opposite of life. All very simple, no doubt—simpler even than our concept—but inconceivable and inexpressible to some poor creature at the whim of centrifugal and centripetal forces. Moreover, even were it possible, one would encounter the twin obstacles of science and cynicism.

Nothing is either large or small, any more than a thing observed first from one end of the opera glasses, then from the other, is alternately large or small. Which in no way mitigates the inevitability of man's birth and death. To live second by second through events that seem to occur one after another, while they actually occur simultaneously and, in literal truth, do not actually occur at all, since the present cannot exist, and that which we call past and future are inaccessible intersections within us. Which amounts to Eddington's eternal present: Events, he says, do not happen; we meet them on our way.

Crazy as it may seem, nothingness or life, emptiness or plenty, these are naive concepts which man erects to overcome his despair of being lost within them, and which he carves like barbarian idols.

Pride constrains some people (at whatever price) to be something, and others to be nothing, while this nothing is just as inconceivable as this something, and this something as this nothing.

I do not refuse to believe that which seems to be. Fine. But if it is, that's another story. As alien to our certainties as is the free and ridiculous magnificence of daydream to life.*

And it is this nothing that remains inconceivable to us, to we who are something, and whose subjectivity is forever embodied in objects. This me and these objects that spring from it are heavy and burdensome weights. We bump up against walls covered in writing, and in order to run from one to another we are compelled to scramble through a furniture storehouse, a junkroom filled with broken statuary, a childhood attic rotten with the skeletons of croquet mallets and hoops. Oh, that we had the agility of dreams, in which we fly so well it seems we can do it even after waking! But prior to sleep, like the three walls that imprison us, we are subject to a whole mountain of objects that block our view of the fourth, which is surely translucent and opens onto countless walls (let us say, onto freedom).

---

*In a dream in which I was pacing up and down before a fork stuck in the ground between the Wallace Fountain and the plinth of one of Marly's horses on the Champs Elyseés, I told myself that I was pacing while *waiting to wake up.* Upon further awakening, I asked myself why I had not lit a cigarette while pacing, as is my custom. It was only then that I realized that *I never smoke in my dreams,* which must have some bearing on my suppression of cigarette smoking in my plays. A suppression I had ascribed to the stopgap nature of smoking for actors, a stopgap that has no place either in a plot or in a text.

Seen from above, a house would seem a highly unlikely place to dwell, were it not for force of habit. Seen from higher up, it becomes a pinpoint. Seen from higher still, it vanishes. From an airplane, human life disappears even before that of its dwellings and cultivations. Soon, life, home, and cultivations have all disappeared.

From higher and higher yet, only the planet's motion can be discerned. From even higher, that will disappear just as the motion of its inhabitants will disappear. It will then seem to have become a solid, motionless and dense, while yet made of this imperceptible and dizzying swarming.

The example works better in reverse. Let us imagine a microscope whose power of enlargement grows stronger and stronger. At first, we see the object, then the matter of which the object is composed, then its spinning atoms, then but a few atoms, then one atom, bombarding itself, then the abatement of that bombardment, then orbs and astral trajectories, then a planet, then a close-up view of this seemingly stationary planet. Then will begin the entire spectacle of what exists on the planet's surface. Then, the dwellings, then the lives and deaths of those who inhabit them.

Seen from close up, then, there exists a house and those who inhabit it. Seen from afar, neither house nor its inhabitants exist. Seen from further still, time recedes like space, to the point of being just a velocity that is finally so fast that it seems to freeze for the ideal observer, in whose eyes this speed has become unbelievable, the centuries following upon one another at such a pace that—after the initial pageant of continents changing shape, oceans swallowing up the land, mountains erupting, islands foundering, and, from a closer view, of temples rising and crumbling, horses, carriages, and automobiles plying the roads, etc. (and all this at the breakneck pace of a sped-up film). From just a little further on, there will be nothing but the sight of a dead world, that has always been dead and always will be, and from a little further on, this world itself disappears, leaving visible only the system in which it turns, and from a little further on, this system disappears, every system disappears, seemingly inert. And all that will be visible—and even this would require a terrifying close-up from the camera eye—is matter seemingly dead.

And while several thousand centuries will have elapsed on Earth since our departure, some phenomenon of perspective, despite the lapse of these thousands of centuries, will reestablish time little by little as we draw near Earth, and will reconstruct the normal perspective of a voyage, in the same way that our approach habitually reconstructs the demolished house and renders it habitable along with all its contents.

It should be understood that this distance, so far and so different from our own, should not be invoked when I speak of those distances that are the aviator's, the astronomer's, or the chemist's concern. The perspectives of the distance I presuppose operate beyond the machinery which, even with science's help, remains perceptible to us. It is likely by force of habit and its own historical conception of the Earth that science refuses to establish a connection between the explosion of which we are but a tiny spark, and the explosions observed under the microscope.

The unknown defends itself masterfully within these phenomena of perspective. First, because a man will answer that he buys a sofa, haggles over the price, has it delivered to his house, sits down in it, stands up, walks away, and returns to it once more. The instantaneous nature of this entire sequence of events would become obvious to him only at a distance that is cancelled out by the fact that any observer capable of observing from such a distance could do so only with the help of equipment that would narrow his field of vision and thereby reestablish the human perspective (whether it were produced by a terrestrial observer, observing other galaxies, or by a galactic one, observing us). He will laugh in my face, then, and tell me I am wrong, and will laugh in the face of any observer or any theorist from any planet. Secondly, if a scientist were to develop such a thesis, he would do so in terms and calculations that would make it incomprehensible to any man going about his life with any degree of self-awareness (while yet bemoaning its brevity). Thirdly, the idea of short and long, of small and large, is instilled in us with such force—with such brilliant stupidity, I might say—as is not easily overcome, except when it is expressed as speculation which the daily newspapers easily defeat by flattering man's pride and his terrestrial point of view.

Man is becoming less and less accepting of his own limitations. He transcends them in his own fashion, which is not always the best. For example, through the use of deadly ultrasonic waves that risk becoming the ultimate weapon in his hands.

Such expeditions beyond our limitations allow us to envision a universal structure that differs considerably from the one that is our creed, and to inquire into problems that are neglected because they disturb our comfort.

I always marvel at the tenuous complacency of scientists. They hold our ignorance in contempt while never considering, for instance, the buffer which cuts them off from inaudible sound. Suffering an occasional bout of blindness before their own domesticity, or before a painter's canvas, would be sufficient to annihilate their smug certitude of being able to pierce this buffer that envelops us and provokes such monstrous errors of moral vision. It is true, however, that the specificity of their field of study necessitates a narrowing of scope.

But even when they move about within their realm with any degree of boldness, they remain imprisoned by habits that prevent us from passing beyond certain dogma and certain relationships. For in passing beyond them, they would consider that they had lost face, crossed over into fantasy, or, to put it plainly, into poetry, with which they confuse it. This must have been what Henri Poincaré (himself a scientist) meant when he told me, one day in my youth at the home of Raoul Duval, that certain experimental subjects yield results that are too peculiar to be useful or to allow us to profit by them.* He added that poets are "very fortunate indeed," but that, lacking evidence, they are not believed.

What does evidence evince? I daresay, it is that reserve, that attitude of circumspection—similar to that of the Church when it is considering a canonization—which cloisters scientists, and has led me to declare elsewhere that science is a laggard and a loiterer.

Man has always sought a confirmation of his own importance in responsibility. One notes that every cataclysm of a cosmic order that has disturbed the Earth seems to him to have been designed to punish some and to save others. He has created his own sort of order out of this disorder. One fellow exploits it in his belief that an angel, or a comet's tail, has swept the Earth to exterminate his enemies, another that it has parted the sea and closed it up again, still another names Pallas the angel of storms, and he becomes the great grasshopper of the Acropolis, his gold and ivory effigy stored in a marble cage. Myriad texts from Egypt, China, Mexico, Lapland, testify to the cata-

---

*The case of Gaston Ouvrieu (1917). He offers proof (uselessly, as far as science is concerned) that it would take very little to radarize the human brain. Ouvrieu is able to drive a car blindfolded at high speeds. He is able to answer questions that his interviewer merely *thinks*. There was no question of a telephathic phenomenon, but simply of a tiny meningeal shell-burst.

clysm—of angelic origin—that threw half the planet into darkness, while seeming, on the other side, to stop the sun in its tracks. All of them interpret it in such a way that man has a hand in it, and none can resign themselves to being but a dust-mote in a hurricane. A society limited in responsibility wishes to think of itself as responsible, because it fears blind force and prefers the supervision of a tribunal, hoping to win the trial yet preferring to lose it rather than to accept a passive role.

The atom is a solar system. Electrons struck by the energy of photons leap from one orbit to another, several times a second. Whereas (says Velikovsky), given the immensity of the solar system, the same phenomenon therein takes place only once in a hundred thousand years.

It is strange that Velikovsky should speak of the immensity of our system and the tininess of the atom's, when both the immensity and the tininess are only relative to us. For the civilizations that exist on atomic planets, the phenomenon would seem to take place at the same rhythm as ours.

Since the cycles follow and subsume one another, it is logical that these texts should record only one cataclysm, the final one before what is to follow (at the same pace) several thousand centuries from now. This self-bombardment of the atomic system allows man a hiatus protracted enough for him to imagine himself on solid ground, and to grow proud of his progress, which the next tremor will reduce to dust. The planet will then move on to new things. It will change structure, discover new Americas.

On Distances

The curious thing is that a hiatus between two regular tremors should allow man himself to induce an unscheduled cataclysm that in no way relates to the rhythm of the atomic quanta. That he should disintegrate his own system while attempting to disintegrate others. Which, between ourselves, is of barely greater consequence.

Man is unaware of the self-bombardment by which our system, like every other, draws the energy for its regular and discontinuous distribution of quanta, since, as I have said, the atom which scientific observation believes to be minute bombards itself several times in a so-called second, and this bombardment, occurring in our world at the same rate, seems to occur at intervals of thousands upon thousands of so-called centuries.

The feeling of motionlessness works in what man calls both directions (large and small). For when the eye draws near to a system, it isolates and uncovers time, as it is revealed to us by our perspective, and when the eye pulls away from a system, it cancels out time, and our perspective reveals matter as apparently motionless, composed of an organization of atoms which he is no longer able to distinguish one from another, and, even more understandably, of which he cannot imagine the machinery. This is why time deceives our senses as to duration, just as it does to sight.

Which proves that time and space are one, and that it is our rules alone that distinguish them. This is as deceptive as a wisteria creeping up a trellis with the ingenuity of a snake, making the human eye mistake it for a piece of inanimate wood.

One proof that time is but a fraud is that a vehicle, managing to leave its system and to enter ours, would see our atomic dust grow into worlds, and its own worlds reduced to atoms as it fled. Returning to its system, it would have to return several thousand centuries after its departure. But—and I have said it before—in rejoining its system, the perspective changes, with the result that, despite the centuries lapsed since its departure, the scales will tip and it will arrive home after the normal lapse of time for such a voyage. On the other hand, if it has the technical capability of viewing our world close up from its home, this *close* will remain a *distant* and it will see nothing but atoms and continuous self-bombardment. This is why man carries within him, in a fairly confused way, conceptions of immediacy and duration whose importunities and contradictions he experiences without being able to discern their cause.

Time will play the role attributed to space, becoming once more the voyager's time, just as, at the plane's approach, his house becomes his house once more, having ceased to be so from his point of view (for which his mind alone acts as corrective); and this house, which had ceased to be a house during his ascent, never ceased to be one for those who inhabit it and wait there for his return.

Let understand who is able. What impedes understanding is that it is too simple. Man complicates everything by starting out on the wrong foot. No doubt what now seems indecipherable would seem decipherable if, by some chance that he was not fortunate enough to have had, he had started out on the right one.

I have already mentioned the phenomenon that seems to differentiate time from space, which is that things from which we move away in space grow smaller, while the things from which we move away in time grow to historical or mythological apotheosis. This time, however, is just another type of space, one of those deceptive distances. The human mind more readily takes possession of things that are temporally distant than it does of things that are, or that we believe to be, spatially congruent. The object that I touch (that I record while deeming less important than some lost valuable) having contours more defined than the object lost and found through the retrogression and the synthetic alchemy of memory.

One might furthermore imagine that we are not even within an atomic system, but on the edge of a cellular explosion within that system, an explosion that would account for the stars' dizzying recession from the Earth that has been noted by astronomers (we being yet engaged in the distance where they have been observed, and thereby able to perceive the explosive recession from which—lacking reference points and thanks to a common projectile speed that is in no way dependent upon the machinery that drives the heavenly bodies—we believe ourselves exempt). I would add that this explosion may not have taken place, but that it *is taking place;* a process which to us appears stable because we would be able to perceive its dizzying explosiveness only from the vantage point of such distance as is inconceivable to man, a dizziness which does not exclude the possibility of a gravitational mechanics driven by acquired force.

Our mistake has always been to believe in our own smallness, which makes no sense, and in an infinity that makes no more, in our duration which is neither short nor long, and in an endless duration which is the same as ours. Infinity, eternity, would then be a ceaseless proliferation of cells of similar proportion and structure, some of which believe others to be either smaller or larger than themselves.

If it should be objected that the preceding chapters contradict me, I will answer that this book is a kind of diary, that I consider contradiction to be the very soul of day-to-day scholarship, and that it is honest not to correct one's errors.

You will tell me that at least this false perspective is our own, that wisdom behooves us to stick to it. That if our senses are limited, we must resign ourselves to them, accept them, and make the most of what they allow. That if man is a cripple, he has adjusted pretty well to his infirmity. No doubt. No doubt, however, that if man were able effortlessly to conceive of time-space as a mirage, he might perhaps rid himself of his hunger for conquest and ruin. It may be true that he would simultaneously lose his will to conquer and to fight. All would then be well in the worst of all possible worlds. Which does not preclude its being good to submit while knowing what it is one submits to, and its being noble to persevere in one's labor while knowing that one's labor is in vain. And, moreover, it is perfectly conceivable that all labor is of equal degree, and that the least of our acts plays a prime role in the machinery.

The life, the death of men and worlds remain a great enigma. It is likely that, here too, there are perspectives. That neither life nor death count for anything. That all things devour each other and mutate in a stillness that is forever an uproarious upheaval silent to us, where neither silence nor uproar are of any more importance than life or death.

Death's mystery lies in its apparent impossibility, since the so-called infinitely small, the distances of which we are composed, should never be able to come to an end.

The limitlessness of the human body is surely based on a duration as indecipherable as our distances, and (in the form of legacy or decomposition, which should not be confused with such poetic turns of phrase as "Flowers grow on graves") the body has a permanence of the invisible, that eternity invoked to glorify the soul. While not forgetting that, when I speak of eternity, such duration derives its meaning only from our distress at our own brevity. I should like someone more qualified than I to examine these contradictions, which would surely cease to be, in some region where our three dimensions would be laughable.

Disengagement from our vocabulary and our code is a work I dare to undertake under the aegis of ignorance. Even if ours is a life sentence, it is better for the prisoner to know that he is in prison. This engenders hope, and such hope is none other than faith.

Ah, how I should love to stop going around in circles, and to know how to orchestrate this chapter. I am, alas, incompetent, but would like it to serve as theme for some scholarly orchestration. I am not up to such an orchestration myself, for the gift I possess is the opposite of intelligence. Alas! It poses as intelligence while bearing a strange resemblance to stupidity. That's my tragedy. I am not ashamed to admit it. Intelligence is not my strong point. It seems to me a transcendent form of stupidity. It complicates everything. Desiccates everything. It is the bellwether that leads the flock to slaughter.

Further, the more my mind grows accustomed to its freedom, and the humbler I become, the more I resign myself to my labor. I refuse to become a raven, brother to Poe's, alighting on some philosopher's bust, and constantly repeating to myself: "What's the use!"

A poet is free not to follow the rails of science. To overcome what's-the-use-ism. One can respect the In-

stitute of Technology and still question its mathematics. Do two and two make four? It's hardly likely, if
I add two lamps and two armchairs. From Heraclitus
to Einstein, enough faulty calculations have accumu-
lated to demonstrate that modern science knows
hardly any more about our world than did the an-
cients, who held it to be supported by an elephant.

As my journey nears its end, the idea of death
comes more easily to me, and seems more to come
down to that state of nullity that was mine before
birth. If we are judged by a supreme tribunal, it is my
feeling that, since the concepts of before and after
stem from our impotence, we are judged as much in
the void that precedes us as in the one that is to follow.
Our actions, ascribable to some breeze that rustles the
fallen leaves, have no effect on that judgment. Human
justice has nimbly substituted itself for any sort of
supreme justice. And I need only see with what impu-
dence it turns its coat, to charge with sacrilege the
earthly judges who would decide the fate of souls.

ON
FRIENDSHIP

Who loves me love I, otherwise none;
And yet, not so: there's nothing I hate,
But wish that all were in the state
Of Good contrived by use of Reason.

CHARLES D'ORLÉANS

The journey we take between life and death would seem unbearable to me without the junctures of friendship.

Love is another fringe of the orders bequeathed to us by nature. Nature's prodigality overabuses the pleasure of an act into which, in order to assure her rule, she drives all and sundry. She seems even to overabuse it against her own best interests, while protecting her thrift through infertile loves. In human jurisdiction, the great caution which nature uses to avoid surplus is called vice. But ideal friendship is a human invention. The greatest of all.

My only politics have been friendship. A perplexing policy in an era when politics, properly defined, serve to divide men, and when one should not be surprised to read, for instance, that Beethoven's Ninth

is a Communist anthem. The preservation of friendships is seen as opportunism. You are required to be in
one camp or the other. You are enjoined to cut your
heartstrings if they extend across the barricade. And
yet, it seems to me that we are partisans of solitudes
seeking to unite. These are fashionable politics no
longer. Opinions bring ruin to emotion, and fidelity in
the face of divergent opinions is an anachronism. As
for me, I am stubbornly persistent, and would rather
be condemned for constancy of the heart than for any
doctrine of the mind.

Unfortunately, the forces I am concerned with
frown on certain invasive friendships that disturb
their work in distracting us from ours. Which certainly explains the length of my mourning list, and
why I have been deprived of the friends who lightened
my journey. Far better to be cautious in relationships.
Whatever my bent for giving precedence to the duties
of friendship above those of my labors, I resist it out of
fear of having to start from scratch, of being punished
for neglecting my solitude in the service of my friends.

Friendship being not an instinct, but an art—an
art that requires unremitting supervision—many cyn-
ics seek to establish its motives as analogous to their
own sexual or monetary interests. Should our friends
defend us against society's traps, society is up in arms,
convinced that their protection stems from self-inter-
est. It is suspicious of disinterest, which it considers a
moot point. Disinterest is praised only in animals,
where it is seen as a triumph of servility and made the
pretext for touching stories and adages such as "the
beasts are better than we are." We are told the story of

a muzzled police dog at Biarritz that saw its young master drowning before his nanny, who was powerless to help him. It found a dog whose jaws were unfettered, and sent it to save the boy in its stead.

A poodle waited every day for its master at the local train station. The master having died very suddenly in Paris, the poodle continued to wait. After several weeks, it allowed itself to die. And the men of that province proclaimed their *awe* by raising a statue in its honor.

Assuredly, I find this statue moving. I love animals and am not insensible to the lessons they can teach us. But the art of which I speak does not govern them. They pledge allegiance to whoever pets or beats them. Man glorifies them so as to glorify himself. Everyone's pet is the most outstanding. This begets mutual blindness.

Friendship requires clearsightedness. It concedes faults to which love is blind. Which is why the friendship of animals is merely love. They deify us, and seek neither to correct our faults by having the courage to correct their own, nor to correct their own so as to set us an example, which is the very crux of the art of friendship.

The poodle's statue is erected to Tristan. Not to Pylades.

True friendship knows no quarrelling, except in the case where the quarrel's magnitude evinces an emotion strong enough to encroach upon love, mimicking its tempests.

In the friendship between Nietzsche and Wagner, Wagner plays the heavy. Nietzsche's neediness remaining ungratified, his disaffection and reproaches play on all that is fair and unfair in passion. This great quarrel is one of love, in that Nietzsche wanted Wagner to become his possession, while Wagner wanted to enslave Nietzsche. Nietzsche, however, sought within the realm of the soul to transcend that bodily commingling through which lovers hope to fuse themselves into a single gasp. The difference of fiber between them shows up at Bayreuth, when Wagner rejects Nietzsche's manifesto for the collection of funds, reproaching the laxity of his call to arms.

Nietzsche's role bears the highest testimony to the soul's feelings of isolation, feelings which a love that leads to marriage could never fulfill. Such soulful passion, alas, is drawn to a feminine nature,† which the world and its pomp lure beyond the tempest. Péguy's letter to Daniel Halévy (*Victor-Marie, Comte Hugo*)†† and the Wagner case have given us two astonishing declarations of love. The slightest grievance bespeaks the passion that dictated them.

I am compelled to wonder whether we shouldn't see in Nietzsche and Wagner yet further evidence of our labors' cold and savage jealousy. Whether we

†Cosima von Bülow.

††Charles Péguy (1873–1914), French poet and essayist, wrote *Victor-Marie, Comte Hugo* in 1910. Daniel Halévy (1872–1962), French essayist, biographer and historian, was the first French translator of Nietzsche. Halévy and Péguy collaborated on *Les cahiers de la quinzane* (*The Fortnightly Review*) and often corresponded on matters of politics, philosophy, and literature. Péguy's *Notre Jeunesse* (*Our Youth*) was written in response to Halévy's *Apologie pour notre passe* (*Apology for Our Past*), which was written in the same year.

shouldn't see in them one of those couples in whom the invisible can no longer tolerate an invasion harmful to its interests, where it mimics those people who are unable to bear the sight of an exclusive understanding. For when friendship grows between two tempestuous beings, one cannot expect the tempest to blow in one direction. Its blast divides itself, and the two new blasts fear being outblown by each other, lest one be reduced to servitude. It is then that friendship finds common ground with love, being at the mercy not only of its germs, but also of the outside obstacles which threaten it.

True friendship does not evolve on such a path. I call it an art because it questions itself, continually sets itself aright, and signs a peace treaty in order to avoid the wars of love.

It is likely that, at those times when I was friendship's victim, my friends were equally victimized because I had strayed from the path. I feel that our labors are otherwise able to accept friendship, if only so as to exploit it. They find within it a means to put us to better use, since friendship drives us to proofs, to believe ourselves responsible for such proofs, to convince ourselves that our work brings rewards that make us worthy of our friends. Means that come undone the moment that friendship oversteps its bounds, that one servitude is added to another, unbalancing our night to the point of disturbing its egoism. In *Tristan and Isolde,* beyond Wagner's love for she who inspired it is the passion he feels for himself, which inspires its passionate style. The work sets forth the relationship formed by certain creators, the fever that wracks this monstrous relationship, whose externally induced fever is nothing but invisibility's screen.

Experience has perfected my skill in this art and in the pains that it inflicts upon us. The encounters that precede its ceremonial should not originate in the thunderbolt, but in the meticulous study of souls.

In this way we avoid stockpiling explosives in our own home.

Friendship alone can find the very simple look or phrase to dress our wounds, wounds which we exacerbate and scratch at with the tenacity of those who, knowing that they suffer from an incurable disease, find an outlet in the extremity of pain. A force equal to our own can do nothing against such wounds, except either to flee, or to lose itself alongside us in our extremity.

Friendship does not seek to inspire. It does not take its pleasure in fanning our flame, in feeding it with gasoline, in conspiring to some magnificent conflagration, in taking part in our downfall.

It observes us without heat. It maintains its balance only to help us maintain ours. At least it is from that angle that I recognize its hard, lovely face.

One can imagine how the lack of spectacle spites a world that lusts for it, and would love to watch, from the comfort of its orchestra seat, our tragic demise. If we do not offer it tragedy, it tries to discover what is hidden beneath a deep concord. It fabricates some conspiracy for it and, having tired of that game, it

bemoans our serenity and abandons us for more tit-
illating drama. The world finds nothing less stimulat-
ing than our serenity under fire. It hopes to be witness
to a massacre. I have often met people who were
exasperated by my reserve in the *Bacchus* affair. They
had been expecting more from it. That I should have
assassinated Mauriac, and been assassinated in turn
by his acolytes. They had no interest in the origins of
the quarrel. They were only interested in the quarrel
itself, hoping that it would eventually bring us before
the courts.

Occasionally, our picadors will turn on victims
whom they had supposed less capable of self-defense.
This is what happened when, thinking they had
wasted their fire on my play, they turned on the Comé-
die-Française's production of *Britannicus*,[1] in which
Marais had performed admirably. The audience had
received the show warmly. But the society of which I
speak wanted to pursue me through him, and riddled
him with jibes in the hope that ours would be a common undoing. This society had not counted on the
friendship which binds us to one another, nor on our
unity of moral outlook. Sure enough, the spectators
were soon bored by this deathless *corrida,* and sought
out other arenas. They train their *banderillas,* their
lances, and their old nags against prey that takes less
time to expire.

The group of composers known as "Les Six"
is a group whose very ethic was grounded in friend-

ship. I was its chronicler. It laid no claim to my ideas, the discipline of which I did not try to foist upon it. Which is why, twenty years later, we found ourselves together again, bound in 1952 by the same common thread, in a little festival that the publisher Heugel promoted from one capital city to another. To date, the blows that had decimated our friends had failed to fall on our group, and should they ever fall, it will not be schoolboy squabbles that manage to sunder it. Friendship brought us together without constraint. Each member blossomed according to his own abilities. We never took the bait of the many attempts made to break us up.

My friendship with Stravinsky is another story, having undergone a sequence of crises. But it always emerged intact, long after society had hoped it was destroyed.

I occupy a fortress whose sentries protect friendship. I have lived in this fortress of friendship since 1949. I am sorry to declare that it will hold fast, and yield only to superior forces against which there is no defense. One marvelous advantage is its aloofness from the great battles. When the great battles draw near, we escape on a boat where friendship sequesters us once more. And if, on occasion, I should leave the fortress to throw myself imprudently into some skirmish, I always return, shutting myself in or fleeing on the boat.

In this fortress, I have found the proof that friendship overcomes the vicissitudes of love, contrarily to that of Triebschen† in which too many conflicting interests created an explosive compound. What am I saying? In which the soul's very fabric disintegrated. Our metal is well tempered, and I have never entertained the possibility of a flaw capable of weakening its structure.

I am not unaware that such a privilege comes dear. I willingly accept the bill for it, knowing the price of good fortune, and that one never ends up paying the incredible price warranted by its worth.

A thousand deadly waves filter through the slightest crack. If we are not to be tainted by mundanity, it is absolutely essential to keep as far as possible from these whirlwinds. Our scholastic, barbaric, and somehow medieval age—with all the power of miracle implied therein—loves to demolish and rebuild. It is both idolatrous and iconoclastic. Marvelous and dangerous, it both consecrates and destroys the individual. One maintains one's balance only within an invisibility whose cunning (for I have already described how invisibility loves to compromise us) consists in making us believe that we are in quarantine and must escape from our hole.

History demonstrates the risk of overestimating the generosity of adversaries who contemplate nothing but our exile. It would be madness to confuse such exile with that which we have chosen—or believe to have chosen—for ourselves, when invisibility

†Wagner's home, near Lucerne, in Switzerland.

makes our decisions for us, profiting by our voluntary exile.

Perfect friendship, the kind that is in no way poisoned by love, feeds itself on forces that are alien to my study. I insist on the fact that, when hidden forces are involved, the borderlines become blurred. And if I speak of an art of friendship, it is of an art that leaves man free, and not of one that enslaves him.

One may well imagine how refreshed I am by this art, after the other, and how pleased I am not to be harried by its shadows. One must only take care not to transgress the rules without which the savage machinery would once again be set in motion.

Having confessed my irresponsibility as an artist, I can concentrate on the responsibilities of my heart. I never allow it to impinge upon my work. There you have it, my judges will exclaim, a life without fire, a life resigned. I must confess to preferring my glowing embers to any blazing fire of delights.

A young chatelaine,* an adopted son, few guests: a rather minimal household. But friendship flows without those explosive milestones that Western ennui sets up along its path to break up the monotony. The tempo of friendship is oriental. The East's mistake was perhaps to have overestimated the West and its syncopations. It was the East that should have sent us missionaries.

---

*Her unstinting generosity taught me to break with the notion of "mine" and "yours," a dismal legacy of the French *bourgeoisie*.

Friendship is customarily confused with *fellowship,* which is its rough draft, and should have been the basis of the *social contract.* And how to account for special friendships? Montherlant and Peyrefitte depict for us the gloom of those makeshift little affairs that develop at an age when the senses are still in limbo and know no forbidden paths.

Fellowships and love affairs have little in common with the attachments of Orestes and Pylades, Achilles and Patroclus. It is a shame that the monks grew suspicious of these attachments, destroying those works of Sophocles, Aeschylus, and Euripides that might have enlightened us concerning them. Greek love, as understood by the moralists, was simply erotic intimacy between pupil and master, and had nothing to do with the powerful bonds of the soul. And if the heroes did happen to overstep the bounds of acceptable behavior, that introduces no new, incriminating evidence into their trial. It is the desire for attachments of this kind that gives fuel to wars, luring myriad men from their bleak, loveless hearths, which they cannot abandon without the pretext of patriotism.

I have kept company with such couples united in fellowship. The failings of the one compounded the failings of the other. One felt the other to be leaning on him for support, while in fact the other was taking advantage of him. Such couples resist through a disorder which they elevate to the heights of fiction. They fabulize themselves to the point of rejecting serenity. They are fueled by alcohol. They end up breaking out in storms, more severe than those of the most tempestuous marriages.

I know a truly amazing story, for which I am sorry not to be able to provide the characters' names, for fear of giving them away.

An architect of Le Havre, married to a lovely young woman, was suddenly possessed by the violent need to dress up as a woman, though there was no element in it of sexual confusion. Being no longer in his prime, his only desire was to become a mature, matronly type. In which he succeeded through the help of one of our friends. He had two apartments, two cars, and a wardrobe of dresses which he ordered and tried on in the dressmakers' shops, where they were completely fooled by his pretense.

His obsession was gratified in conversations with his accomplices, in whom, for instance, he would confide: "I should marry. I should find myself an older man who won't be interested in me for my money." His young wife suspected nothing, and would certainly have been more hard-pressed to accept the truth than some genuine perversion.

The charade lasted five years, after which his double life became burdensome to the architect, compelling him, as a man, to ruin himself at the gambling table for the female persona to whom he would subsequently revert.

He killed himself in his feminine abode. Stretched out on his bed, dressed as a man, he held a letter in which he had written: "I ruined myself for myself. I thereby ruined the wife whom I adore. I beg her forgiveness."

That was a singular pair. It sums up pretty neatly such fellowships in which neither love nor friendship can claim to take part.

Being familiar with my contemporaries and my compatriots, I am sometimes obliged to warn young people that they risk being the subjects of gossip by associating with me. Incredibly, the fear of hearsay causes them to shrug their shoulders when they meet with those who seek it. Such people pretend to fear gossip, while by their cunning they lay themselves open to it. They will not hesitate to sully either themselves or us, in order to bask in the notoriety of being our intimates.

Youth must be respected above all, and as respect is not easy to come by, people make no effort to understand youth's heartfelt exuberance, which they willfully malign.

Any police report will show this to be true. I don't advise anyone to get involved in that sort of thing. A society such as ours is ignorant of all subtlety of heart and soul, going in for humiliating interrogations and treating as mentally ill those whose embarrassment causes them to speak poorly in their own defense. Such embarrassment is seen as evidence of guilt. They blush. That is evidence enough for indictment and the shameful infliction of a medical examination. I have known cases in which the poor victims were unable to endure their shame. They took refuge in suicide, thereby providing the police with false evidence of their guilt. It's deplorable. And even in those cases where there is a bent towards so-called perversity, the subject is overwhelmed with the anxiety of being considered outside the norm, and of being cast as a monster by his family.

In this second instance, the repressed instinct ended in tragedy. From one humiliation to the next, from one analysis to another, the victim was able to find no other sanctuary than in death.

We do not aspire to change the world. That is up to science. Our efforts at enlightenment will persuade only the righteous, who are already persuaded.

It remains to declare the aim of this paragraph: To speak to those who read me as I would if they were sitting before me.

I have noticed that even the most clear-thinking minds are influenced by the indecent idiocies retailed by the press. It is never vain to try to enlighten them a little. Of course, I do not mean to defend myself. I know of nothing so vulgar as those who defend themselves or who boast of defending us. I have great admiration for Mme. Lucien Muhlfeld, who was accosted in her own home one day by a young lady, who declared: "I have just been out defending you." We watched as she kicked the young lady out, enjoining her never to return.

People do not realize that it is impossible to defend those we love, for the very good reason that those who love us should not associate with those who slander us. And if they do associate with them, their attitude alone should be enough to silence them. I flatter myself that a slanderous mouth cannot be opened before me. Should such a mouth be opened, I leave the table or the room. Let people babble all they want in my absence. In my presence, let them shut their traps. That is one precept of my ethic. And to the best of my knowledge, I have never allowed myself to lapse in it.

The Walt Whitman business has nothing to do with loving friendship. It deserves a category of its own. It is in camouflaging Whitman that his translators incriminate him. And of what? He is the rhapsodist of a kind of friendship in which the word *fellow* might bear its true meaning. His hymn far surpasses back-slapping. He sings a union of forces. He controverts the very junctures which Gide confesses. It is a shame that, in trying to defend a poorly known region, Gide gives us only its bare outlines. Wilde idealizes it with worldly elegance, and Balzac, too—in offering Wilde (with the Vautrin-Rastignac dialogue that takes place in the garden of the Pension Vauquier) the model for the Lord Harry-Dorian Gray dialogue that takes place in the painter's garden—offers us a force face-to-face with weakness, a weakness that bursts out when, at Camusot's house, Rubempré reviles his benefactor.

Proust sets himself up as judge, and the beauty of his work loses much meaning thereby. We can only lament that his passages on maniacal jealousy do not shed any real light upon us.

Let us return to the crux of our chapter, friendship, vestal virgin of the fables with which society adorns it. It ennobles both men and women, though women may be more prone to jealousy than men. Whereas jealousy has no role in friendship. Quite to the contrary, friendship consists of serving emotions that are alien to its compass. It neither suspects, nor watches for, nor lays itself open to reproach. Its role is rather to see for those whom love's extravagances have blinded, to help them both in happiness, should they find it, and in misfortune, should they feel its blows. This said, friendship should use extreme caution in meddling with love; if it fails, its support may appear to be expediency in the interests of self-preservation.

I receive a great many letters offering me friendship. People are surprised that I don't jump at these offers, and that I answer such enthusiasm with reserve. I shall answer now. The art of friendship may be summed up in the Chinese dictum, "Constrict your heart," which does not mean "suppress the use of your heart." It means, rather, "Do not step outside the chalk circle." It has taken me a long time to develop the friendships with which I am comfortable. One more and the circle will overflow. Such wisdom does not suggest that I triple-lock my door. My door remains wide open. Only, it is not the door to my treasury.

Man is very quick to use the word *friendship,* to caress and be familiar, to the point where the least of circumstances brings this fine edifice tumbling down. I preserve my true friendships, except when death steps in. And if I should add new friendships to old, my first care is to instruct them on a past of which they have no knowledge. In this way, old and new are able to join seamlessly, and the new are not compelled to remain aloof.

The metal of friendship claims itself to be imperishable. I could cite friends whom some have tried to delude about me, and who know very well whether or not I am capable of uttering such words or of performing such actions as have been attributed to me. And that, only if they allow me to be spoken of behind my back, which should not be, but which sadly is. For my part, I avoid such back-stabbing like the plague, and having set this slanderous bent to rights, I notice that I have disappointed the company, who would have preferred me to come sliding down the chute alongside them.

One should not believe friendship exempt from the test of inclement weather. This book has recorded several drenchings. I have spoken of the long study that should precede friendship. The clear-sightedness this study bequeathes, contrarily to love, should open our eyes the minute friendship begins to go bad, but that is not easy since it is indulgent and would rather overlook failings. But if such failings seem to grow not out of shortcomings but out of excess of sensibility, disorder sets in without one's noticing it. The element of luck enters into the balance of true friendship. No one's nature is impervious to a jarring shock that issues it unforeseen directives. When such a shock is not forthcoming, it is only by a stroke of luck comparable to that of a gambler who wins several times in a row at roulette on the same number.

Nevertheless, in the long run we see the light. We lend lady luck a hand in such a way that we can make use of her without cheating.

The work of friendship would be too easy if it were always able to avoid the obstacles which the work of art, calling out its invisible guards, puts in our way. Even more so, considering that we must perform both together, never confusing one work with the other, and never allowing our labor to think itself envied by friendship.

A fortress is almost indispensable to maintaining this most unsteady balance amongst the merry-go-rounds, parades, shooting galleries, roller coasters, and swings of the city.

I would recommend to friendship that, like wine, it should not allow its bottle to be shaken. Besides, friendship hates being disrupted, even for a moment. In this, it is comparable to the triad whose disruption unleashes catastrophe. For example, it would rather travel in company so that, in the case of accident, it runs the risk of common death.

The Bishop of Monaco tells me that he is responsible for a young lady's death in the Languedoc disaster. She had been so impatient to leave that he gave up his seat to her. This is the bishop of a rock on which rises a temple—the temple of Fortune. The bishop had not been this young lady's friend. He had only been doing her a favor. Had he been her friend, he would undoubtedly have liked to take to the air by her side.

In an age of bustle and headstrong spirits, friendship is considered useless. What is friendship to one who would sacrifice it on principle? What is friendship to a world that spits on refinements of the heart? I don't give a damn, as they say. He who cries last, cries longest.

P.S. I know that it is immodest to talk about oneself. Many great examples of this are available.* But this book is addressed *to friends*. It will fall from the hands of those whom it rejects. And it is normal to speak with one's friends without the slightest constraint. The machinery of which this book is a very awkward study will soon repulse anyone whom it doesn't want eavesdropping. In the final analysis, this is what made me recognize that I was less free in writing it than I had thought. I have ended with the chapter "On Friendship" because it is to friendship that I speak.†

---

*"Custom has made a vice of speaking of Oneself . . . Those are calf-bridles with which neither the Saints, whom we hear speaking so highly of themselves, nor the philosophers, nor the theologians fetter themselves . . . thus, let he who would be known give himself boldly to be known by his own lips."

Montaigne

†Cocteau originally intended to make "On Friendship" his final chapter. In *Past Tense,* he writes, "I am not yet dictating my book. I may have to finish it in the Greek islands. Maybe add a chapter on *Oedipus Rex* and the meaning of the masks . . ." (p. 156).

Perhaps the outline of my ethic will show through this disorder, the disorder of a man groping in the dark, and will put attentive souls on their guard against the danger of delirious wandering. There are things allowed us, and things that are not. I should have loved to write brave, delicious books. Whatever it is that dictates such books does not poison their authors. The future alone, if there is one, will pass judgment on my imprudence. It is true that I should suffer more in trying to be prudent.

I have never been prudent, for which I can claim no fame since I don't know what it is to be so. I dive headlong into my actions, come what may. Erik Satie describes how, as a young man, he was forever being told: "One day, you'll see." "I am fifty years old," he told me, "and I have yet to see a thing."

There is a custom amongst certain families to say that some money is being held aside for us, that we should not touch it, but save it in case "something should happen." They forget that something—life—is continually happening to us, and that we are dying at every moment just as surely as we will die for good one day.

ON
A WAY OF LIFE

Take care not to shave your antennae of a morning.

Respect movements, flee schools.

Do not confuse progressive science with intuitive science, the only one that counts.

Do as the beautiful woman: see to your figure and your petticoats. Though, of course, I am not speaking literally.

Be someone else when receiving your blows (Leporello).

People would say to Al Brown: "You are not a boxer. You are a dancer." He laughed at this, and won.

Do not take up cause against the inaccuracies printed about you. They are your protection.

Be a constant outrage to modesty. There is nothing to fear: modesty is exercised only among the blind.

One is either judge or accused. The judge sits, the accused stands. Live on your feet.

Never forget that a masterpiece is testimony to intellectual depravity. (A break with the norm.) Turn it into action, and society will condemn it. That is what usually happens anyway.

Contradict the so-called avant-garde.

Hasten slowly.

Run faster than beauty.

Find first, seek later.

Be helpful, even if it compromises you.

Compromise yourself. Obscure your own trail.

Withdraw quietly from the dance.

He who is affected by an insult is infected by it.

Understand that some of your enemies are amongst your best friends (a question of standards).

Fight any instinct to be humorless, for humorlessness is the worst of all absurdities.

Do not fear being ridiculous in relation to the ridiculous.

Don't put all your baskets in one egg.

See your disappointments as good fortune.

One plan's deflation is another's inflation.

A certain kind of stupidity is essential. The encyclopedists are the source of the kind of intelligence that is a transcendent form of stupidity.

Do not close the circle. Leave it open. Descartes closes the circle. Pascal leaves it open. Rousseau's triumph over the encyclopedists is to have left his circle open when they closed theirs.

The pen should be a dowser's rod, capable of reviving an atrophied sense, to help an infallible yet almost totally dysfunctional sense. (The real me.)

Do not flee yourself in action.

Allow the power of the soul to grow as flagrant as the power of sex.

Kill the critic within. Be persuaded only by that in art which speaks violently to the sexuality of your soul. By that which elicits an immediate and spontaneous moral erection.

Expect neither reward nor beatitude. Return noble waves for ignoble.

Hate only hatred.

An unjust conviction is the supreme title to nobility.

Disavow anyone who provokes or accepts the extermination of a race to which he does not belong.

Understand that those who judge us know nothing of the mechanics of our work and attribute it to mere capriciousness.

Be a mere assistant to your unconscious.

Do only half the work. The rest will do itself.

Avoid all thinking that attributes inner labor to some mysterious, exterior influence.

Consider metaphysics as an extension of the physical.

Know that your work speaks only to those on the same wavelength as you.

Anything of any importance cannot help but be unrecognizable, since it bears no resemblance to anything already known.

Fear idolization like the plague. The idol will be covered over, the non-idol uncovered.

Written numbers speak to an inferior level of intelligence. The poet's politeness consists of *not writing his numbers*. The great pyramid expresses itself solely through relationships. The ultimate politeness in art consists of speaking only to those who are able to uncover and measure its relationships. Anything else is symbolic, and symbolism is merely transcendental imagery.

The wall of stupidity is the handiwork of the intellectuals. One disintegrates trying to get through it. But one is compelled to get through it, regardless of the cost. The more basic your equipment, the better its chance of overcoming the wall's resistance.

CONCLUDING LETTER

My dear Bertrand,

Please forgive this little treatise of "unlettered science." It is an exhausting hide-and-seek in which men refuse to participate, preferring their own games. Which often tempts us to imitate Heraclitus, and sink back into playful childhood.

Perhaps we are finites, containing finite systems that contain others, *ad infinitem*. Perhaps we all dwell within one of these finite systems (which would be perishable) that are themselves contained within perishable finitudes. Perhaps this infinity of finitudes one within another, this Chinese box, is not the kingdom of God, but God himself. Our duty would then be to recognize our scale (in which creatures hop up and down like frogs in a bell jar). Not to lose ourselves in disheartening perspectives.

Everything burns and consumes itself. Life itself is the result of combustion. Man's contribution is to leave behind himself a trail of lovely embers, some of which remain glowing; through these embers the past is revealed in the form of presence; it can be seen a little in its true aspect. For these embers (or works) draw on an imperceptible human essence that is not subject to our standards of measurement.

Since they will be here tomorrow when we no longer will be, they must overlap with what we call the future, giving us a vague sensation of fixity, of permanence.

A medium's excavations in the so-called future yields objects that are no less out of context than the Etruscan vases from the so-called past that are so easily dug up in Ostia. That is what we find so disturbing when faced with the little oracle of Delphi. Motionless, stable, his toes lined up neatly in a row, he seems to have come from the depths of centuries past, continuing on his unmoving way, carrying the white cane of the blind.

He has always struck me as representative of the deception practiced by the perspectives of time-space. He has left an arm, his chariot, and his team of four behind him. But team of four, chariot, arm, all testify as much to unforeseeable gestures of the future as to unrememberable gestures of the past. To me, he stands for the *eternal present,* of which he is an exquisite, astonishing little milestone.

POSTSCRIPT

During my last visit to Greece (12–27 June, 1952) to verify figures for *Oedipus Rex,* I carried in my pocket your letter on the scale which Pythagoras and China invented together, without knowing it. Here are my notes on *Oedipus Rex* and on my journey.

ON
AN ORATORIO

Jocasta has just hanged herself. The plague is raging. Everyone has gone indoors. Thebes closes its shutters as a sign of mourning. Oedipus remains alone. He is blind, he is not seen (sic). . .

At Colonus, he said: "I did this." I stayed in the dead center of the room. My eyes could not bear the disgusting brilliance of that chandelier.

MYSTÈRE LAIC†

Any serious work, be it of poetry or of music, of theater or of film, demands a ceremonial, lengthy calculations, an architecture in which the slightest mistake would unbalance the pyramid. Unlike Eastern spectacle or sporting competitions, however, in which figures and architectures draw on a code that is familiar to the public, ours answer to rules that are ours alone, and cannot furnish proof of excellence.

The work of *Oedipus Rex* was not easy. I could not overwhelm the ear with the eye. I had to be violent, yet respectful to the monstrous mythology. Truly, myth comes to us as silently as a flying saucer. Time

†Jean Cocteau, essay as part of *Essai de critique indirecte* (1932).

---

and space send it from some planet whose customs are alien to us. I disturbed Igor Stravinsky's oratorio neither by spectacle nor by dance. I was satisfied with seven brief scenes that occur, while my text is performed, on a stage high above the orchestra. It would be inaccurate to claim that I was inspired by the Japanese Noh. I had simply remembered its exemplary economy of gesture and allusive power. I marvelled at the workers' understanding that allowed me to create the masks. Nothing, no matter how strange, can put them off when there is a problem to be solved. I might add that the wars of 1914 and 1940 have dug a trench which permits the young not to worry about whether or not something has been done before. In contrast, we have done and seen too many things not to be obliged to try new ones. For if we are no longer young, it is important that our works should be. *Oedipus Rex* dates from 1923. In 1952, it has become a celebratory ritual for the reconciliation between Stravinsky and me, after so many years spent apart.

Album du *Figaro,* June–July, 1952

It was only in Vienna, up on the stage at the edge of a forest of instruments, facing that crowd crammed into the stalls, boxes, and galleries, and applauding Stravinsky through me, that I had any real sense of the spectacle that I had been unable to bring to Austria† and which, in the Champs-Elysées Theater, had gone on without my being able to see it,

†Cocteau's elaborate scenarios for the 1952 revival of *Oedipus Rex* could not be transplanted from Paris to the Vienna Konzerthaus.

behind my back. I had followed it in the audience's gaze. I was finally able to see it at the Konzerthaus, free from anxiety, no longer having to wonder if everything was running smoothly, all obstacles removed. The impression hit me so strongly every time I turned around on stage, pushed forward by the conductor, lashed by waves of applause, that I was able to forget the absence of any spectacle. I thought of myself as an audience that had seen it. This sensation was, I repeat, enhanced by the fact that, never having seen the show myself, having measured it only by the great layers of shadow and light which the raising and lowering of the curtain cast on the audience, I was able to believe that it had always been invisible, that my inner tension alone had communicated it to the room, like that of a hypnotist. Vienna, therefore, *had seen it* through hypnosis, and by the time of my fifteenth curtain call, I had become convinced of this. The regrets later expressed to me regarding the absence of spectacle, and the explanations required of me, awoke me from my own hypnosis. I decided, in order to allow myself to see it, to put in writing what I had told the Viennese. More than any workings of spectacle, *Oedipus Rex* represented for me Mont-Boron, Stravinsky and his family, my youth, all those things of which I speak in the chapter "Birth of a Poem," as if the time that separates that chapter from the one I am writing did not exist, and I were writing them consecutively. This came undoubtedly from the sensation of having Stravinsky at my elbow, and that memory substituted its own theater for the one in which I played the role of narrator.

If I record these memories as I did for my ballet *Le jeune homme et la mort* in *La difficulté d'être,* it is because productions tend to evaporate, to crumble, to go to ruin. Of all those I have staged, I have not one photograph to remind me. Nothing is left of the *Roméo et Juliette* at the Soirées de Paris. I had invented, together with Jean and Valentine Hugo, the darkness in which nothing was seen but the colors of the arabesques, the costumes, and the scenery. Red lighting, placed on the outer edge of the stage, prevented the audience from making out anything else. Invisible footmen erected streets and interiors around the actors' choreographed movements. I had devised a very peculiar gait for the entire youth of Verona. Romeo alone did not walk in this exaggerated mode of behavior.

But where melt the snows of yesteryear?

The masks of *Oedipus Rex* were fashioned so as to be seen from below. Seen head on, they were unreadable. Most were ovoid, studded with eyes stuck on the ends of cones or rods. The hairpieces were made of raffia. Cork baffles, wires, and cushions, set off from the surface, were used for noses, ears, mouths. From the final mask sprouted sheaves of corn topped off by ping-pong balls painted red. What in the south would be called *semble-sang*—mock blood.

Gestures never quite becoming dance, and making scant reference to mime, were essential in maintaining the balance between masks and orchestra. For the wearer of a mask, the raising of a hand or the stride of a leg takes on great importance, in the way that a violinist's arm resolves into sound. The fact that an arm seems smaller next to a mask isolates it and magnifies it fourfold, not in size but in visibility. Furthermore, we could not use costumes. We had to suggest costumes on a foundation of unadorned black tunics. I allowed them to be hung with coarse material, but in such a way that these cascades did not obliterate the lines of the body. Otherwise, my actors would no longer be actors wearing false heads, but dwarfs with enormous heads. I did not make the same mistake as in *Le boeuf sur le toit,* a mistake into which I had dragged Dufy, and which Picasso had pointed out to me. Each of my false heads was of a different size and structure. The final, massive mask for blind Oedipus was emphasized with the white balls of his daughters' heads, and the oval figures hung from the chorus' instruments.

The work took us through a month of preparation and a month of manual labor from my artisan assistants. Laverdet on the curtain and the finishing of the masks. Villat on the set design. Mme. Bebko and her son on certain special masks, such as the horse and jackal heads, the figure of Athena as grasshopper with her green crest. The rest was done with anything found at hand (nails, old bulbs left lying around by a photographer) and with the consummate skill of Laverdet's assistants, who were able to grasp the ungraspable even before it was explained to them. It is important to visualize that the show was staged high up and far off, that not only was I required to leap the proscenium, but also the entire orchestra and the chorists. My only annoyance was having to turn my back on the stage and being unable to watch what was going on. I kept myself informed by watching the audience, of which I had a wonderful view from the proscenium and which, with the rare exception of some incurably stupid face, was most striking in its immobility.

DESCRIPTION OF THE SCENES

I
The Plague Arrives One Night in Thebes

The plague, enormous, its great, round, microbic head pale green, was seen crossing the stage, from left to right, before three young Thebans made of one man with outstretched arms and two masks. At the far left, a large, realistic moon pushed along a tulle shadow, from left to right, turning the young man in the center towards the plague, after he had dropped his two masks. He approached the plague, kneeled, made a salutation, and took in the crook of one arm draped in red a death's head which he attached to his own face. He moved off towards the left, was seized in a fit of trembling, fell doubled over to the floor, stretched out, and lay still. Then a second young man, emerging from the lunar mechanism by a stairway on the far right, saw the plague, bowed, and donned a death's head, taken in the crook of his left arm draped in black. He trembled, and the curtain fell on this episode.

II
Sadness of Athena

The curtain rises, revealing two pale blue struts painted with line drawings of Pallas Athena, face to face and backwards, composed of a 7, a 4, a 0, a 1, and *part* of a 3. These struts are held up from the outside by two men with the heads and tails of black horses. A sky blue pediment, inscribed with an eye, descends from the rafters to crown the two struts, leaving a small empty space between the tops of the struts and the bottom of the triangle. When the pediment is in place, Athena climbs the central stairway that opens out behind this frame, or temple-like structure, and stops on a pedestal. Her face is that of a green grasshopper, surmounted by a helmet with a green crest. In her right hand she carries a spear, in her left a green shield on which a cruciform relief simulates the face of the Medusa. This shield is surrounded by writhing serpents. A double-ended spiral spring mimics the eyes. Dangling from the spring is something vaguely resembling a human outline.

Athena leans her forehead against the spear (a left-right profile) while stepping onto another, black pedestal. Then she turns her head, presenting it in a right-left profile. Then she grows still, facing ahead, raises her left arm and hides her head behind the shield. Medusa's head becomes her own. The curtain drops.

III
The Oracles

The curtain rises, revealing three people. In the center, raised up on an invisible cube, is Tiresias, draped in a yellow robe and black coat. He has three heads, one facing ahead, two in profile. The two profiles rest on the actor's shoulders. To his left, back to the audience, is Jocasta. Oedipus' head the shape of an egg. Jocasta's head the shape of an ellipse. They turn to face the audience. Tiresias' hands are wrapped around his own throat, to the right and to the left of the central mask. Jocasta, then Oedipus, pull white ribbons from the mouths of each of Tiresias' profiles. They move off, stage left and right. When they have reached the far left and far right, the ribbons break away from the shadowy mouth, and they pull them in with their right hand (Oedipus) and their left (Jocasta). They wave them about, then lay them, Oedipus against his heart, Jocasta against her belly. Then they let them fall to the ground and they spread their open hands. Tiresias' hands return to their original position. The curtain falls.

IV
The Sphinx

The curtain rises on a long, low, terra-cotta-colored wall, painted with black zigzags on a white background. To the right and to the left, at each end of the wall, stand two jackal-headed men. Near the jackal on the left, we see the Sphinx in profile, facing the jackal on the right. The actor walks backwards. He wears his mask (head and chest) on his back and his neck. His extended arms are hidden by white wings. He lifts his knee, and we see the bird's tail attached to his left thigh. The Sphinx opens his hanging wings and spreads them. The wings tremble. He beats them slowly, moving towards the right end of the wall, which conceals the actor's legs. There he stops, lifts his left knee and shivers his wings. The curtain falls.

V
The Oedipus Complex

The curtain rises on a group of three actors in black tunics. Two of them on one knee, a leg extended. They are wearing half-moon masks in which black profiles are set off against a light blue background. The half-moons are brought together to form a full moon. Behind them, standing on a cube, the third actor wears a mask which is the iris of an eye set at the center of the body of a white fish. The actor, his arms crossed, is wrapped in a dark blue cloth. He lets the cloth fall. Immediately, the half-moons break away from one another and the actors wearing them move off to the right and to the left. They turn about, revealing a second profile. Once again facing the audience, they execute gestures, along with the central actor, that consist of drawing the numbers 1, 3, 4, and 7 in the air. They are wearing white gloves. The central figure finishes with the gesture 0. The curtain falls.

VI
The Three Jocastas

The curtain rises on an empty stage and, to the right of the central stairway, a dog composed of two actors, one standing, jackal-headed, the other bent over, holding his partner's waist. A long black tail completes the silhouette. The third actor comes down the central stairway, carrying in his arms a mannequin representing the corpse of Jocasta the Mother. The actor sees the dog, backs away, turns, and scrambles up the stairs. Hanging by the neck from a red scarf, Jocasta the Wife is lowered from the rafters, her right hand spread across her belly. Her foot dangles below her robes. Immediately, the unoccupied actor reappears from the stairway on the right. He is wearing the large head of Jocasta the Queen. Its mouth is open, from which flows a long band of red material. The dog moves off to the left, followed by the head-bearing actor. Dog, actor, and red band comprise a procession that files past the mannequin's dangling feet. The curtain falls.

VII
Oedipus and His Daughters

The curtain rises on two actors, to the far left and far right, in black tunics, rigged up in equipment similar to that of a glazier, from which are hung the chorus' masks. From the central stairway, we see descending the great mask of blind Oedipus. When he is completely revealed, he stops. His hands rest on the egg-shaped heads of his daughters. Beneath each egg hangs a little dress, one of pale mauve, the other of pale blue. Oedipus kneels, gathering his daughters to his chest. The choruses approach and take his daughters from him. They move off. Oedipus rises. He makes imploring gestures with his left arm. The chorus to the right returns to Oedipus and replaces his young daughter beneath his hand. Oedipus then turns about, his daughter moving from his left to his right. We now see nothing but Oedipus' black-mantled back, his hair, the red sheaves of his eyes, and the egg with Antigone's pigtail. The group moves onto the stairway. It begins its climb while the curtain falls.

We might have feared laughter for this final, bizarre, and aggressive scene. But it was as if the audience were paralyzed in a panicked stupor. We attributed the atmosphere of silence, and the clamorous applause that followed the final curtain, to the fact that I had pushed my style to its very limit. Stravinsky's shadow, conducting the orchestra, added to the solemnity of the whole. One can hardly begrudge the journalists who saw nothing but grimace and caricature, since even Charles Maurras treats the primitive heads in the Acropolis Museum as nothing but Barbary apes.

The backdrop was a vast painted cloth (dominated by greys, mauves, beiges, and sulfur yellow) inspired by one of my drawings for *La machine infernale:* blind Oedipus and Jocasta on a jumble of overturned steps.

ON
A TRIP TO GREECE

The traveller fell dead, stricken by the picturesque.
MAX JACOB

The bizzarre nature of the fact alone compels one to say it: Greece is an idea one develops, and develops endlessly beneath a sky that lends itself to this kind of illusion, to the point where one wonders whether Greece even exists, whether we exist when travelling there, and whether all its islands and its Athens where the peppermills fill the air with their pepper, are not simply some fable, a presence as strong and as dead as that of Pallas Athena, for instance, or of Neptune. One wonders, climbing like a goat over the bones of kings, embalmed by those immortals in whom the storm unleashes a web of odors as alive and as extinct as that oracle who walks, his feet motionless, through the centuries, his gaze like the white cane of the blind. An idea built up and destroyed, immortal and mortal, like those immortals who desiccate beneath the sun around the cave where the sibyl prophesied and before her door where the Sunday crowd lined up. An idea, yes, an obsession, so obsessive that it remains standing on its oracle's feet, watching us with an eye that sees us not. And this eye of an idea sends out its gaze over everything, over Delphi, crowned with its dead theater, over Crete, where we were nearly lost in the open labyrinth of Knossos that conceals ideas of red bulls and bees, to which the hillside hives, and the waists of princes and princesses, mercilessly crushed against the walls and bloody columns, bear witness. Over Santorini, which escapes its volcano only by a white flight to the summit of its lava peaks. Over that idea, the idea which the sea chews like cud, over and over, to the point where it mumbles, over and over, to the point where one would sacrifice one's daughter to silence it, to calm its mumbling upheaval of one's boat, which is an idea of a boat, and would float better on that river where heroes are no more than shadows of themselves than on the sea. And in that idea of an infernal place, those ideas of men and women marry, copulate, give birth, and choke up memory with their progeny. Here is an idea, a crazy idea, one of those ideas that are medically treated in the clinic parks crammed with travellers who look just like us. Here is that inaccessible Greece. One enters it by some unknown crag or cave, seeking the dog Cerberus, lost by its master, who compels Hercules to find it again, and to steal oranges, and to do Augias' housework, and to drain the Lernean swamps, everything resolving into three-headed dogs, or hydras, or rivers to be diverted, or golden apples, and one believes it all because the mouth that tells it never lies, but instead accuses History of mendacity, History which is not an idea but a procession of dead actions strewn across the stage-boards. We had to acknowledge this idea, since we were inside it, ideas ourselves that were as one with the idea that contained us and became our very substance. And how to leave it, without, like Ulysses stuck to his seat, leaving a part of ourselves behind? This seemed impossible, since the winds kept changing and blocking our escape. What am I saying? An idea of wind, akin to those young sons of Boreas who, tired of Hercules' hunting stories, stuck him on an island where he called for his young companion in a cry unbearable to the nymphs, who had just drowned the boy, and who plugged up their ears. Another idea which became that of Ulysses and confounded the idea of siren-song. Great gods, what to do and how to escape this circle, and won't the trumpet-playing angel appear and with his idea of a trumpet wipe out our daydream and overturn the polar axis, as he did on the day of King Ajax's funeral, vanishing after he wiped his mouth? For the angel was an idea ready to vanish on the heels of another, and quite a one it turned out to be, that usurping idea, a cataclysm recorded in the Bible and which Saint John had the notion of eating in the form of a book on the island of Patmos,† which, being so much an idea in the air, we had no notion of visiting.

We had no notion to sail on the Ionian Sea, and if we had, the only way to have gotten out of it was by another idea, the idea of an eagle, which grew as the idea Zeus had formed of his own power, and extenu-

---

†Cocteau writes in *Past Tense,* "A bell-boy of the Patmos-Palace Hotel went crazy. He screamed: 'I am John,' and devoured the hotel's guest register" (p. 157).

ates Xerxes' idea of lashing the sea, Caesar's idea of insulting the river, the Thracians' idea of shooting arrows at the sky. And what good would it do us to take refuge in a museum, since there we would lose ourselves amongst the trees of the forest of Medusa's victims, and the broken branches of these trees would find some way of grabbing us with the idea of hands? Oh, how terrible it is, and how many tourists are not even aware of it, who by their lack of ideas miraculously manage to resist the idea that is smothering them. We noticed this at the theater of Dionysus, whose erotic ideas could not contaminate the female visitors, who were protected against all ideas by the tour guide and by their impermeable suits. The mere fear of being medusaed by that sequence of ideas, by the goddess' deadly shield, was enough to make us wary, which we were, and which I remain, and the idea of Greece haunts me still through the long night of that sleep which destroys men and spares only ideas.

NOTES

The notes provided in this translation do not represent scholarly research or interpretation. They are merely intended to provide the curious reader with titles and publication information for major works cited in *Diary of an Unknown* that are available in English translation.—*J.B.*

ON INVISIBILITY
1. Jean Cocteau, *Cock and Harlequin*. Translated by Rollo H. Myers. New York: Henry Holt & Co., 1927.
2. Marcel Proust, *Pleasures and Days*. Translated by Louise Varese, Gerard Hopkins, and Barbara Dupee. New York: H. Fertig Pubs., 1978.
3. Marcel Proust, *Within a Budding Grove*. Vol. I of *Remembrance of Things Past*. Translates by C.K. Scott Moncrieff and Terence Kilmartin. New York: Random House, 1982.
4. Jean Cocteau, *Opium: Diary of a Cure*. Translated by Margaret Crosland. London: P. Owen Pubs., 1957.
5. Jean Cocteau, *Les Enfants Terribles*. Translated by Rosamund Lehmann. London: Folio Society, 1976.
6. Jean Cocteau, *The Infernal Machine*. Translated by Albert Bermal. Norfolk, CT: New Directions, 1964.
7. Jean Cocteau, *Orpheus*. Translated by Carol Martin-Sperry. New York: Grossman Pubs., 1972.

ON THE BIRTH OF A POEM
1. Jean Cocteau, *Oedipus Rex*. Translated by e.e. cummings. New York: New Directions, 1963.

Notes

ON CRIMINAL INNOCENCE

1. Jean Cocteau, *Bacchus*. Translated by Mary Hoeck. New York: New Directions, 1963.

ON THE DEATH PENALTY

1. Jean Cocteau, *The Blood of a Poet* [film script]. Translated by Carol Martin-Sperry. New York: M. Boyars, 1985.

ON A PURPLE PASSAGE

1. Jean Cocteau, *Professional Secrets*. Translated by Richard Howard. New York: Farrar, Straus, Giroux, 1970.
2. Jean-Paul Sartre, *The Devil and the Good Lord*. Translated by Kitty Black. New York: Random House, 1962.
3. Jean Cocteau, *The Eiffel Tower Wedding Party*. Translated by Dudley Fitts. New York: New Directions, 1963.
4. Paul Claudel, *Tête d'Or*. Translated by John S. Newberry. New Haven: Yale University Press, 1919.
5. Stendhal, *The Charterhouse of Parma*. Translated by M.P. Shaw. New York: Penguin, 1958.

ON PERMANENT LADIES

1. Pierre Corneille, *The Cid*. Translated by John C. Lapp. Arlington Heights, IL: Harlan Davidson, 1955.
2. Heinrich von Kleist, *Prince Friedrich of Homburg*. Translated by Diana Stone Peters and Frederick G. Peters. New York: New Directions, 1978.

ON A JUSTIFICATION FOR INJUSTICE

1. Jean Cocteau, *The Typewriter*. Translated by Ronald Duncan. London: D. Dobson, 1947.
2. André Gide, *Lafcadio's Adventures*. Translated by Dorothy Bussey. New York: Random House, 1980.
3. André Gide, *Two Legends: Oedipus and Theseus*. Translated by John Russell. New York: Vintage Books, 1950.
4. Jean Cocteau, *Antigone*. Translated by Carl Wildman. New York: Hill and Wang, 1961.
5. André Gide, *Isabelle*. Translated by Dorothy Bussey. New York: Vintage Books, 1931.

Notes

6. André Gide, *The Counterfeiters*. Translated by Dorothy Bussey. New York: Random House, 1973.
7. André Gide, *Les Caves du Vatican (Lafcadio's Adventures)*.

ON TRANSLATIONS
1. Jean Cocteau, *The Human Voice*. Translated by Carl Wildman. London: Vision, 1951.
2. Jean Cocteau, *The Eagle With Two Heads*. Translated by Carl Wildman. New York: Hill and Wang, 1961.

ON MEMORY
1. Jean Cocteau, *Paris Album 1900–1914*. Translated by Margaret Crosland. London: W.H. Allen, 1956.
2. Jean-Paul Sartre, *Saint Genet*. Translated by Bernard Frechtman. New York: George Braziller, 1963.

ON DISTANCES
1. Jean Cocteau, *The Difficulty of Being*. Translated by Elizabeth Sprigge. London: Owen, 1966.

ON FRIENDSHIP
1. Jean Racine, *Brittanicus*. Translated by George Dillon. Chicago: University of Chicago Press, 1961.